HEAVEN
AND # HELL
UNVEILED

HEAVEN AND HELL UNVEILED

Updates from the World of Spirit

by

STAFFORD BETTY

www.whitecrowbooks.com

For information, contact White Crow Books
at 3 Merrow Grange, Guildford, GU1 2QW United Kingdom,
or e-mail to info@whitecrowbooks.com.

Cover Image Mysterious Encounter. Copyright © by Rassouli. All rights reserved.
Cover Designed by Butterflyeffect
Interior design by Velin@Perseus-Design.com

Paperback ISBN 978-1-910121-30-6
eBook   ISBN 978-1-910121-31-3

Non Fiction / Body, Mind & Spirit / Death and Dying

www.whitecrowbooks.com

To my wife Monica,
my daughter Southey,
and sons Louie and Sam

Also by Stafford Betty:
Vadiraja's Refutation of Sankara's Non-Dualism
The Rich Man
Sing Like the Whippoorwill
Sunlit Waters
Thomas
The Afterlife Unveiled
The Imprisoned Splendor

Contents

Introduction

Imagine yourself an agnostic Jew. Since your bar mitzvah you've pretty much stopped practicing your religion. You never give God a thought and never pray. You don't believe in an afterlife. You're a "cultural Jew." If it turns out there is an afterlife after all, what would happen to you? Would you "go to hell"? Or imagine yourself an evangelical Christian. You love Jesus, accept him as your savior, and feel assured of your salvation. You sing in the church choir and seldom miss a Sunday service. When you die, what would happen to you? Would you "go to heaven"?

It might surprise you to learn that there are research-based answers to these questions and that these answers almost certainly don't match what you've been taught.

Beings who speak to us from the afterlife present a very different picture of heaven and hell. I'm a university professor specializing in afterlife study, and I want to assure you that not one of the dozens of accounts reaching us from the Other Side that I've studied speaks of the afterlife in the manner described above. In fact they renounce this view and warn against it. We'll see why a little later.

What the "dead" are telling us—I'll usually refer to them as "spirits" or "our spirit friends"—is that the answers provided by earth's religions are simplistic and often seriously misleading. These spirits see things more clearly than we do, and this clarity gives them an advantage that we lack. Speaking for myself, I find their perspectives enriching and often inspiring, vistas to be marveled at and imitated. I have read a great deal of theology and spiritual literature over the course of a long life, and much of it has been helpful, but most of it doesn't match up to the spirit classics I'll introduce you to here. Plato compared our world to a dark cave, and St. Paul famously said we view things here "through a glass darkly." These remarks resonate with me when I read spirit literature. No thoughtful human being who has ever wondered about the meaning of life and our destiny beyond death should miss it.

But how do "the dead" speak to us? Five years ago, if I'd said they speak through mediums, many readers would have rolled their eyes and wondered how a well-published professor of religion could take such "nonsense" seriously. We've come a long way since then. Scholars have begun sorting out the spurious and fraudulent from the legitimate and worthy. My 2011 book, *The Afterlife Unveiled*, is an example. The list of books on the afterlife is growing exponentially, and most of them are based on otherworldly accounts reaching us through mediums. What distinguishes them is that they are based on actual experience rather than an ancient scripture or theological reasoning. In my view our spirit friends—the legitimate ones—should be regarded as earth's most trusted spiritual teachers.

I hope you are interested. As for me, when reading the most inspired of these narratives, I experience a high that almost lifts me out of my office chair into that world they speak from. That is really saying something, for I am no mystic, no medium, no saint. I'm an aspiring seeker and a pretty good researcher. And I can tell you this with some assurance: We are all about to enter a fascinating world. And the more we know about it, the less scary death will be—at least if we are basically decent people. So let us sit for a few hours at the feet of the dead, some of whom left earth hundreds of years ago. We will never look at heaven and hell the old way we used to. Our religion, if we have one, will be changed. Everything will begin to make more sense than it ever did before.

1

The

Sources

The books I've worked with and will be introducing you to were composed and channeled in the last 160 years. About half come from the British Isles, which seems to be a hot spot especially loved by those among the dead who yearn to tell us about their life on the Other Side. This is not surprising, for the British have shown a uniquely strong interest in the afterlife since the founding of the Society for Psychical Research in London in 1882. In fact one of the most famous accounts of afterlife conditions came from one of the founders of the Society, Frederic Myers—after he died, of course. His earthly interest appears to have "carried over."

But why honor these other-world sources as legitimate oracles? There are several reasons. First, the great majority of legitimate mediums assert emphatically that they are not the source of what comes through them; the spirits are. More importantly, many of the best narratives are full of what researchers like myself call "evidential." For example, if the spirit speaking or writing through the medium shows intimate knowledge of conditions on earth that the medium would not be expected to know, that's "evidential." British and American psychical researchers working a century ago created thousands of "book tests" to assure themselves that invisible intelligences, or spirits, really were the sources. In a typical case the spirit would reveal, through the medium, what is on a particular page of a particular book in the library that had been his before he died—and there, when checked, it would be.

Some of the best proofs of legitimacy are technical and can be found in various books written by my colleagues, especially by my good friend Michael Tymn.

One of the indicators of legitimacy that has most impressed me over the years is the consistency of the accounts. The many reports written by spirits from England, France, the United States, Brazil, India, and elsewhere corroborate each other. If I've read 30 of these accounts, I can be pretty sure what the 31st will say. I don't mean in their particulars, for each spirit is unique, and astral matter responds easily to each spirit's imagination, but in their generalities. This congruence suggests to me that they are describing a real world, and that the descriptions are not, with some exceptions, figments of the mediums' imagination.

I say "with some exceptions" because we know that mediums have to work hard to keep their minds pure receiving stations and that they don't always succeed. If they don't, the thoughts of the spirits will be "colored" or "contaminated." We know that "coloring" sometimes happens because the spirits themselves complain *through their mediums* that their intentions are being misrepresented. "Get your biases out of the way so I can come through clean!" the spirits say in effect.

It's because mediums do sometimes fail, despite the best of intentions, that it's important to sample many accounts from different mediums before coming to any conclusions. If you put your faith in only one medium, you could be seriously misled.

Even though I've read over a hundred reports by many mediums, I'm not so arrogant as to claim I've got everything figured out. To begin with, I trust some and distrust others. One of America's most popular mediums has been caught cheating, and I make a point of avoiding her. Others I'd almost bet my life on. In general, trying to put a face on the afterlife can be likened to spying in a foreign country. You learn to trust some sources far more than others, but you're seldom absolutely sure you've got everything exactly right. When the sources agree on anything, especially when they all do, you know you're on the right track. That's what I'm always looking for. What you have here is the fruit of that search.

In spite of my broad knowledge, a knowledge that I feel secure enough about to share with the world, I expect to be surprised when it's my turn to shed the body. In fact, the spirits themselves tell us they can only approximate the majesty and wonder (or in some cases the horror) of their world through the homely speech of mortals. They also tell us they are far from omniscient. All they can do is point us in the right direction.

2

Dying

What is dying like from the point of view of our spirit friends? And what immediately follows dying?

One of the richest descriptions of the afterlife was transmitted from the mother of an Anglican minister, Rev. Vale Owen, in 1917. Owen's mother had died eight years earlier. The book, *The Life Beyond the Veil,* was first published in 1920. In it is a moving description of a passing that vividly suggests the difference in attitude between typical earth-side views of death and the spirits'. Bear in mind that the speaker is the Rev. Owen's deceased mother. Here is the full account.

We once were sent to a large town where we were to meet with other [spirit] helpers at a hospital to receive the spirit of a woman who was coming over. These others had been watching by her during her illness, and were to hand her over to us to bring away. We found a number of [her earth] friends round the bed in the ward, and they all wore long dismal faces, as if some dire disaster was about to happen to their sick friend. It seemed so strange, for she was a good woman, and was about to be ushered into the light out of a life of toil and sorrow and, lately, of much bodily suffering.

She fell asleep, and the cord of life was severed by our watching friends, and then, softly, they awoke her, and she looked up and smiled very sweetly at the kind face of one who leaned over her. She lay perfectly happy and content until she began to wonder why these strange faces were around her in place of the nurses and friends she had last seen.

She inquired where she was, and, when she was told, a look of wonder and of yearning came over her face, and she asked to be allowed to see the friends she had left.

This was granted her, and she looked on them through the Veil and shook her head sadly. "If only they could know," she said, "how free from pain I am now, and comfortable. Can you not tell them?" We tried to do so, but only one of them heard, I think, and he only imperfectly, and soon put it away as fancy.

We took her from that scene, and, after she had somewhat gained strength, to a children's school, where her little boy was, and, when she saw him, her joy was too great for words. He had passed over some years before, and had been placed in this school where he had lived ever since. Then the child became instructor to his mother, and this sight was a pretty one to see. He led her about the school and the grounds and showed her the different places, and his schoolmates, and, all the while, his face beamed with delight; and so did the mother's.

A very different death scene awaited those who died on the Titanic in 1912. It was vividly described by one of the passengers who died, W. T. Stead. Stead had been a champion of Spiritualism and a medium in life, so he was well prepared for death. Here is his description:

The whole scene was indescribably pathetic [or sad]. Many knowing what had occurred, were in agony of doubt as to their people left behind and as to their own future state. What would it hold for them? Would they be taken to see Him [God]? What would their sentence be?

Others were almost mental wrecks. They knew nothing, they seemed to be uninterested in everything, their minds were paralyzed. A strange crew indeed, of human souls waiting their ratings in the new land.

A matter of a few minutes in time only, and here were hundreds of [spiritual] bodies carried through the air, alive; very much alive, some were. Many, realizing their death had come, were enraged at their own powerlessness to save their valuables. They fought to save what they had on earth prized so much.

6

The scene on the boat at the time of striking was not so pleasant, but it was as nothing to the scene among the poor souls newly thrust out of their bodies, all unwillingly. It was both heartbreaking and repellant. And thus we waited—waited until all were collected, until all was ready, and then we moved our scene to a different land.

A final death scene comes from Winifred Coombe Tennant, an upper–class Englishwoman communicating through the celebrated Irish medium Geraldine Cummins in 1958. Her passing was perhaps typical of what ours will be like. She died in old age of natural causes and seems to have been a conventionally good person of no particular distinction

> After I woke up from the sleep of death, and following its uneasy dreams, some pleasant, some nightmares, my father and mother appeared to welcome me. Then your father [she is writing to her son through Miss Cummins] and my sisters came. But my end was my beginning. I was too overjoyed at getting a glimpse of George, your brother, so father and mother soothed me, calmed me, took charge of me and gave me my first sense of locality and environment.
>
> It was all rather gradual—time of oblivion and unawareness, then those two were there beside me—my parents almost like doctor and nurse, and they guided me back into real consciousness.

What is perhaps most interesting in these accounts is the reuniting with loved ones and the absence of a judging God. Earth's two largest religions give no hint of such a passing. Islam says that two angels of death interrogate the newly deceased in their tomb a day or two after their death, and most Christians expect to be judged by God and sent to heaven, hell, or purgatory within minutes of their death. Nothing remotely like this happens. Yet, as we will see in a later chapter, there is a judgment. But it doesn't unfold the way most of us have been taught.

Note also the presence of spirit helpers in the first and third accounts. It's one of many ways that spirits render loving service to each other. You might say it's part of their religion.

Perhaps the most important lesson here is that we don't really die when we pass. We just shed the physical body and keep going in a spiritual, or "astral," body.

3

Their World

The Englishman Rev. Drayton Thomas communicated with the dead for over twenty years through the highly gifted medium Mrs. Osborne Leonard. The main communicators were his father, John, a Methodist minister, and his sister, Etta. John died in 1903, Etta in 1920. Both proved to be particularly gifted subjects. Between 1922 and 1940 Thomas published seven books dealing with the subject of survival. Much of the communication—the best part of it—came from John and Etta. Often father or sister passed on information about other spirits they had come to know. All in all, they describe a wide spectrum of characters and geographies. We'll look at those in just a moment, but first a warning from John:

There [on earth], as here, each views life from his own standpoint, and personal preference guides attention towards one thing and away from another; this play of individuality shows itself conspicuously in communications from beyond death.

> There is another fact which makes such descriptions vary; all who speak are not dwelling in the same part of the next world. Some are in supernal light, others in dim borderlands where they remain until improved character refines their senses and so makes possible an advance to brighter realms. Just as a Laplander's account of life on earth would differ from that given by a Zulu, so does life present wide differences in The Beyond.

In a short chapter in Thomas's most popular book, *Beyond Life's Sunset,* John and Etta describe their world, with occasional help from other spirits. Often Drayton Thomas leads the discussion with questions.

"Does your world appear to you to be solid and similar to this one?" I asked my sister after she had been there for some few years. She replied: "Yes, it is a place as earth is, and looks like it. It is a place, a similar world, but with greater opportunities and affording us greater knowledge. I know how difficult some people must find it to realize this."

My father, alluding to my mother still on earth, said: "I have a home there, with a garden and flowers. They are real flowers. Your mother will be glad to see this, it is a real garden with actual flowers."

Shortly after my head gardener passed on he described to me some of his first experiences, and among them this: "They took me out and showed me a garden, some of the flowers and plants I knew as well as I know my own name. It was familiar and seemed to make it all very natural to me. . . . We walked along looking at the trees and hearing the birds sing and I noticed a building that looked as if made of beautiful stone with lots of roses climbing over."

My father sometimes gives descriptions thus: "I often take long walks. The soil seems different from that of your earth, and I notice less variety of surface. Our ground is more like natural soil, but without mud or anything disagreeable, and it is springy and pleasant for walking on. With us the dwelling places are not too close together and we have no such closely populated districts as on earth. We are able to travel easily over great distances but I walk at times from choice. So much that seems fanciful and wonderful to you is fact with us. . . ."

There is evidently something about the atmosphere which makes a vividly agreeable impression on those newly arrived. A friend who in his old age had been very sensitive to cold alluded to it thus: "Where I now live it is so beautifully bright and in every way delightful. One does not see the sunshine pouring on you from a round object [like the sun], and yet one feels as if bathed in a glorious sunshine. We have no nights and I have not seen it even dull; it is always light. I can understand now why, in references to this life, there has been so much mention of light, actual as well as symbolical." . . .

Here is my sister's description of her surroundings: "Our houses are very much like houses on earth, except that one is not condemned to live in a house which one does not admire. I have seen occupants in houses which I knew they would not like after a time, but it was because they chose it as being like theirs on earth. So I cannot say that every house is a dream of beauty; a house may have been chosen because it reminds of family ties, of old happenings, and other earth associations. Yes, everything looks the same as on earth. I do not think of anything which looks different from its kind on earth. But we have no rain, no night nor darkness, no sun nor moon. You might think that some people would miss that, but the effect of them is present; we have a sunshine which seems to originate in our atmosphere, and which is far more satisfactory than being dependent on clouds and wind...."

An elderly lady of my congregation talked to me as follows some years after her passing: "I was rather relieved on finding that I could still have pretty things and nice furniture on coming here. God's wisdom is so wonderful in providing for us, not only on earth, but here. Many who realise that God has provided good things on earth do not think He has done so here; they talk much about rest, 'Gone to his long rest' they say, not knowing that we just step from one condition to another, a better one if we are ready for it. I found it pleasant to still have walls and furniture around me; it was easier to take up my spiritual work because of those familiar conditions, easier that it would have been amidst strange ones. My home is not built of brick, of course, but still it looks like brick, and the furniture and pictures are as solid to us as is your home to you. We can manufacture such things by thought. But not big things at first, it takes some time to learn how to do that. We still use our hands as well. In higher realms they can do it all by thought. On the lowest they do nothing by thought." . . .

My father and sister spoke of welcoming G.M., who had been a lifelong friend.

Describing his awakening they said: "He has been rather surprised to find how extremely natural it all is here. At first he could scarcely realize it, but on the whole it has been a great relief to him. It is intensely interesting to welcome people like G.M., for besides the pleasure of having them with us, there is the extraordinary interest of observing their surprise on wakening. They always exhibit relief at finding themselves in a tangible world. Many people fear death owing to an idea that they are about to exchange the tangible for the intangible. It is not fear of finding themselves in a bad place, but rather a dread of the unaccustomed. In this case G.M. was particularly pleased to find tangible things and people around him and scope for activity."

A few weeks later this friend was again spoken of: "G.M. is now getting on remarkably well and quickly picking up the new conditions. He is most interested in everything. He has now ceased to question the reality of what he sees around him. At first he was inclined to say: 'Well, what I see cannot be really present'. But after a short while he had to admit that so many different things could not exist merely in his imagination and that the most vivid dream could not go on so long. He tells us that, having now relinquished that mental attitude, he feels pleased and enthusiastic about everything, and insatiable in his desire to see and know more. He says that again and again he stops to ask himself, 'Why did we not know this while on earth?'" . . .

I once pointed out to my father that many people would question, on reading his descriptions, whether his world was as actually real as ours here. He replied: "There is something in that. While speaking I felt how bald and bare was my description compared with the reality of that world. Yet, there are grass, trees and flowers, as well as other forms with which you are not familiar, things of which I cannot give you any conception. I hope that occasionally some spring may be touched during our conversations which will suggest helpful comparisons. Remember how, sometimes unexpectedly, you are touched with sudden happiness, an extraordinary uplift, illuminations and hope, and yet you are unable to tell others why. Really, you are then sensing the hidden hope in life; that world which is hidden from you is revealed *to* you, the eye of the soul beholds that which the physical eye cannot see. Now, as we go on and upward, we increasingly perceive the hidden beauty, love and hope in all things. It is not so hidden from us as it is from you. Etta and I are in a marvelous world."

After reading many similar accounts, I've come to the following conclusions about the afterworld based in part on research summarized in my earlier book, *The Afterlife Unveiled*.

1. Our present ideas about heaven and hell are illusory. Hell is hellish, yes, but it's not a place of physical pain, nor is it everlasting, nor is it a place where there is not help. And heaven is not one place but a spectrum of worlds stretching from the lowly joys of souls newly arrived to spheres of unimaginable bliss and perfection for souls far more advanced. The afterworld is not some fantastic vision of infinity where souls are locked in poses of permanent rapture gazing at the face of God. And no one floats on a cloud while playing a harp. Rather it is a place with landscapes and seas and houses and cities reminiscent of our own world. It is an objectively real material world, but made of matter vibrating much more rapidly than our senses can pick up. There are gardens, universities, libraries, and hospices for the newly dead—but no factories, fire stations, sanitary landfills, or smokestacks. There are no dirty jobs to do. "We have no traffic, and our roads are covered with the thickest and greenest grass, as soft to the feet as a bed of fresh moss. It is on these that we walk," says the spirit of Msgr. Hugh Benson communicating through the English medium Anthony Borgia. He is describing a relatively low zone of the afterworld sometimes called Paradise or Summerland. It resembles a glorified earth. This is the plane described above by John and Etta Thomas.

2. The afterworld begins at the earth's surface and extends outward. Earth is the nucleus of the entire world system that the spirits describe. "The spirit world begins very near the earth and extends millions of miles beyond," writes the spirit of Leslie Stringfellow, a Texan who died at 20 and communicated through his parents. It "surrounds yours on all sides, like the atmosphere does the globe, and every nation has its counterpart in spirit, surrounding it, in connection with that part over or nearest its earthly place of residence." Many spirit communicators tell us that their world "envelopes and interpenetrates the physical world"

3. Spirit realms vary from culture to culture. Stringfellow described what he called "foreign trips": "We went yesterday for the first time to a part of the Spirit World occupied by Turks and Hindus." We should not expect the Eskimo's afterworld to look like the Maori's. The laws governing their worlds will be the same, but the appearances will vary. Nor should we expect Sunni and Shia Muslims to be living comfortably side by side in the same sector of the afterworld—or Han Chinese entrepreneurs and Tibetan peasants. Physical violence is not possible in the afterlife, but old habits of mutual suspicion and animosity don't disappear just because we die. Progress takes time, both here and over there.

4. Earth's slow "vibrations"—we don't have a scientific understanding of what this word means, but it turns up everywhere in spirit communications—dumb down our ability to sense the presence of spirit, including the Divine. A quickened "vibration," such as we find in the afterworld, or what we'll sometimes call the astral, greatly increases one's sensitivity to spirit. The Divine is no closer to the astral world than to our own, but spirits can discern or intuit the Divine more cleanly.

5. The newly "dead" are thoroughly themselves when they pass. Their personalities and habits and character, for better or worse, are completely intact. Nothing miraculous happens to them when they pass. Their astral body is not a "resurrected" body, but was always present as the soul's "inner envelope" while embodied in earthly flesh. Once the physical body dies, the inner body quite naturally becomes the outer—as a snake's inner skin becomes the outer skin once it sheds the old. There is nothing miraculous about the process of surviving death.

6. So natural is the process of dying that many souls do not realize at first they have died. One spirit said, "I groped my way, as if through passages, before I knew I was dead. . . . And even when I saw people that I knew were dead, I thought they were only visions." That is because the difference in appearance between the physical and the astral body is relatively slight; so is the difference, as we've seen, between the new world they've entered and the old one left behind.

7. Life in the afterworld is more vivid and intense than on earth, not more ghostly. Spirits often describe their world as more real

than ours: Our earth is the copy or facsimile of theirs, theirs is the prototype. Astral beings have fewer limitations. They can communicate telepathically and with much greater precision than through the cumbersome medium of speech. They can move from place to place by willing to be at their destination, though they can walk if they want to. Their minds are sharper, their emotions more acutely felt, both positive and negative. They see and hear as before, but in a more intense way. On the other hand, they may be no wiser or morally better than they were before. And they are far from omniscient. "I cannot tell you when your grandson will next require new shoes," W. T. Stead wrote through his medium to his sister Estelle, "nor can I tell you the settlement of the Irish question." Spirits don't get the answers to all the questions that puzzled them back on earth just because they've "died."

8. Some spirits describe a phenomenon known as the akashic or etheric records. These records contain the history of the places they cling to. The spirit of David Patterson Hatch, communicating through the American medium Elsa Barker, gives an example: "I have been in Constantinople and have stood [in spirit] in the very room where I once had a remarkable experience, hundreds of years ago. I have seen the walls, I have touched them, I have read the etheric records of their history, and my own history in connection therewith." These records "lie layer against layer everywhere." The spirit of Professor Ian Currie, communicating beginning in 1992, says that the akashic records reveal in detail the pasts of all souls but are kept in a realm far beyond the humbler realms of souls newly come over.

9. The afterworld is composed of astral or etheric matter, which is "largely malleable by thought," as one spirit put it. Another stated that it could be "manipulated with infinite ease." Benson describes the complex but swift erection of a building out of astral matter by "master masons": "nowhere were there to be seen the usual materials and paraphernalia associated with earthly builders, the scaffolding and bricks and cement, and the various other familiar objects. We were to witness, in fact, an act of creation—of creation by thought—and as such no 'physical' equipment is necessary." So prominent is thought creation in astral matter that Judge Hatch describes spirit life as "both subjective and objective." In other words, what you think you see in the outer environment may in fact be a construction of

your imagination that you project outward, either consciously or subconsciously. The construction will stay in place until you dismantle it with a followup act of imagination.

10. The old or decrepit or injured bodies left behind at passing do not have to follow spirits into the next world. The physical leg that was shortened by polio can be instantly restored to normal size. The damaged brain no longer need cage the spirit. The wrinkled old body can be young again in its astral vigor. "The healers and physicians on the astral plane," says the spirit of A. D. Mattson, communicating through the English medium Margaret Flavell in 1972, "concentrate their treatment on making persons realize that their illness is only in their minds and that the mind is influencing the astral body, producing the simulated illness." The mind has full control over the body if only the mind realizes it—a degree of control denied us earthlings.

11. The afterworld provides opportunities for every wholesome interest or avocation—from science to music to theology to astral architecture to homebuilding. It is a joyful, endlessly fascinating place, full of challenges, for those mature enough to value it.

12. Physical danger does not exist in the astral. Neither does physical illness. Eating is optional and sleep unnecessary. The calls of nature do not even get a mention. Spirits may retain their outward appearance, but the inner composition of their bodies (their organs) is of no consequence and (from what I can deduce) altered.

13. There are hellish regions in the astral, and large populations that make their home there. The Shadowlands are a vast world of many conditions. The landscapes vary from sordid city neighborhoods to parched, gray scrubland to dark, lifeless deserts. The vivid clarity of higher realms is missing. Instead there is a dull overcast. Temporarily lost or confused or stubbornly unrepentant souls populate these regions. Disturbing noises and howls are sometimes mentioned. Frances Banks, communicating in 1965 through the English medium Helen Greaves, gives us a horrifying picture of a Nazi leader (not Hitler) who committed suicide when Germany fell. The man, now remorseful and eager to pull himself out of his personal hell, "was a terrible and pathetic sight" with soars and scars and sightless eyes—all of which he imposed on his astral body by the power of his subconscious mind.

14. There is duration, but nothing like clock-time with its schedules and deadlines. Three months after her death, Banks wrote, ". . . already my experience of earth and time is fading. I seem to have been here for aeons." Seeking to demystify those of us tempted to think of the afterworld as timeless (as many of us have been taught), Hatch reminds us that time is nothing but sequence, and that as long as past and future exist, there is time. He explains that in the afterworld "one may find a silent place where all things seem to exist in unison; but as soon as the soul . . . attempts to examine things separately, then sequence begins." Events in the afterworld, other than those enjoyed during meditative states when one experiences "union with the All," are sequential. Thus there is time.

15. Spouses, relatives, friends, and former teachers, some from earlier lives, some long forgotten, turn up and may renew old friendships. If two persons linked by love to each other on earth want to continue the relationship after death and are, roughly speaking, spiritual equals, there is nothing stopping them. Ties that were deep don't disappear with death.

16. Many spirits are members of large spirit families, or "Group Souls," that await them when they pass. They feel as if they have come home when they are received by the familiar group. Banks tells us that souls in a Group are "part of ourselves. Their connection with us is deeper and far more permanent than mere earth contacts could make it."

17. Spirits are not naked, but clothed. Astral clothing is fashioned by the mind, usually without any conscious effort. Clothes are actually part of the astral body. After analyzing hundreds of spirit communications, Robert Crookall concluded that a spirit's clothes "automatically reflect his character because they are part of the total self—part, in fact, of the subtle body that automatically responds to his habitual thoughts and feelings." There are no clothes closets in the astral.

18. Children of all ages are raised in the afterworld. They are not magically transformed into adults just because they died prematurely. One of the noblest professions in the astral is nurturing and educating spirit orphans. Great numbers of spirits are engaged in this satisfying form of work.

19. There is plenty of time for relaxation and play, especially for children, who enjoy many games. Laughter is often reported. Jokes are told. Ecstatic joy is not uncommon. Spirits even enjoy hobbies, knitting being one of them. "Do not be shocked. Did you fancy that a lifelong habit could be laid aside in a moment?" said Hatch. There is plenty of time in the astral. Raymond Lodge, a young man killed in 1915 in the First World War, said that "thousands and thousands" would be visiting their earth homes on Christmas. Of course, they visit unseen, and the lack of welcome can bring sadness—but also a clearer grasp of their situation.

20. Animals are often mentioned by spirits. "It is perfectly true that all the dogs that we've had in our family I can find here," says Mattson. "They are still individualized." But dogs no longer loved "have gone back to the group soul and have added their quota of affection, love, and devotion, to be used again when other dogs come to earth." A few spirits mention wild animals. The adventurous young Texan, Leslie Stringfellow, discovered in his astral travels "another part of the Spirit World set apart for the use of wild animals that were wild on earth. They still seem afraid of men. Their forest is vast and dense and there are thousands of all kinds of animals that existed on earth ."

21. Would you expect to find an advanced science in the Afterworld? As early as 1913, Vale Owen's mother describes a colony of scientific institutions with its many spirit scientists and instruments. She then gives way to a more evolved spirit, Astriel, who presents a picture of the universe undreamed of by earth's physicists:

What we want you to understand is that there is no such thing as blind or unconscious force in all God's Kingdom of Creation. Not a ray of light, not an impulse of heat, not an electrical wave proceeds from the sun, or any other star, that is not the effect of a cause, and that cause is a conscious cause; it is the Will of some conscious being energizing in a certain and positive direction. These beings are of many grades and many species. They are not all of the same order, nor all of the same form. But their work is controlled by those above them, and these are controlled by powers of still higher grade and sublimity.

Astriel doesn't contradict any of the findings of modern science—he is completely comfortable with evolution and the universe's vast scale, for example—but he adds to the picture. What scientists miss—spirits working behind the scenes—he supplies.

Spirits regularly tell us that most of the great ideas behind earth's inventions are inspired by spirits telepathically communicating their ideas to those we call geniuses.

The universe that channeled literature describes is not micromanaged by an almighty God. The Infinite Source leaves all that to spirits, from the highest to the humblest, from the creator of a habitable planet to the inspirer of a musical composition. Zabdiel tells us, "There are manifold classes of creation—mineral, vegetable, animal, human, terrestrial, solar, and stellar. Beyond this, also, the stars are grouped together and dealt with by hierarchies qualified for that great task." A stupendous picture emerges from this literature. Why things run this way will become apparent as we explore life in heaven, to which we now turn.

4

The Divine Source

In Somerset Maugham's great novel *The Razor's Edge*, the lead character, Larry, tells us about a conversation he had at a monastery in France. He asked why God created the world, and the monks told him "for his glorification." Larry was troubled. "Did Beethoven create his symphonies for his glorification?" he wondered. "I don't believe it." Though deeply attracted to the "splendour of the services," he ended by rejecting the monastic life and turning away from Catholicism.

So why *did* God—or the Infinite—create the world? What is the best answer that earth's saints and sages come up with? St. John of the Cross puts it as well as any human can: "God's purpose is to make the soul great." Rabbi David Wolpe makes the same point when he describes us as "spirit buds." If we are buds today, tomorrow we may be flowers. Nothing less could please the theist's God so much. For God's innermost nature is loving, and love desires the good of the beloved – just as the best and wisest of human parents desire nothing so much as the good of their children.

This is perhaps the best we can do from our lowly perch as we wonder and hypothesize about the intentions of the Infinite Being. Our spirit friends support us—then go beyond us.

One of the most striking portrayals of this Being comes from a spirit calling himself William James, the great American philosopher and psychologist. The style and brilliance of intellect as they reach us in 1977 through the renowned American medium Jane Roberts are strongly suggestive of James, but who can say for sure? In any case, we see the psychologist in "James" right from the start:

> Nowhere have I encountered the furnishings of a conventional heaven, or glimpsed the face of God. On the other hand, certainly I dwell in a psychological heaven by earth's standards, for everywhere I sense a presence that is well-intentioned, gentle yet powerful, and all-knowing. This seems to be a psychological presence of such stunning parts, however, that I can point to no one place and identify it as being there in contrast to being somewhere else. At the risk of understating, this presence seems more like a loving condition that permeates existence, and from which all existence springs.

He goes on to say,

> I am convinced, then, that this atmospheric presence is the creative medium from which all consciousness springs. . . . More, this light is surely the same that in another fashion lit the skies of Boston, dawned over the ocean, and splashed upon my study floor. But the quality of this knowing light differs, for it is alive with a loving intent that is instantly felt and experienced in a direct manner. There is no mistaking its intent, and again I am struck by the ambiguity of its vastly personal and impersonal aspects.

James then points a condemning finger at the materialist who denies the world of spirit and leaves us feeling "alienated from God and man, alone in a chaotic universe, a creature accidentally thrown into existence like a live coal from some gigantic furnace, sizzling for an instant with the cracklings and rustlings of desire, but soon reduced to ash." James shows himself elsewhere in the book to be well acquainted with the science of the day, but he doesn't hesitate to denounce the conventional wisdom: "To imagine that such an entire environment [earth] is an accident is, I see now, intellectually outrageous as well as emotionally sterile." His view of atheistic materialism is typical of all the channeled accounts I've read. Few of them fail to warn us of its dangers to the human spirit.

Spirits don't speak of seeing God in some celestial humanoid form. Many of them explicitly rule it out for beings at their level. Vale Owen's mother says that "God is not more visibly present here than He is in earth life." Frances Banks tells a spirit child that God is "Much too far away for us even to see Him. We're not ready for his glory yet." When Drayton Thomas asks his father if we will ever be able to see God, John Thomas answers, "I do not think that, as you develop and progress, you will wish to see Him. You will not wish to limit Him in that way. . . you would have brought Him down, made Him into a Being only one-millionth part of that which He is." And Imperator, a highly advanced spirit speaking through the gifted Anglican minister Stainton Moses around 1880, put it to us with some tough talk:

> But though we have not yet seen Him, we know yet more and more of the fathomless perfections of His nature through a more intimate acquaintance with His works. We know, as you cannot, the power and wisdom, the tenderness and love of the Supreme. We trace it in a thousand ways which you cannot see. We feel it in a thousand forms which never reach your lower earth. And while you, poor mortals, dogmatise as to His essential attributes, and ignorantly frame for yourselves as being like unto yourselves, we are content to feel and to know His power as the operation of a Wise and Loving and All-pervading Intelligence. His government of the universe reveals Him to us as potent, wise, and good. His dealings with ourselves we know to be tender and loving.

Maurice Barbanell, a practicing British medium for over fifty years until his death in 1981, channeled a spirit calling himself Silver Birch. Silver Birch described himself as a "messenger of an advanced group who used the astral body of an Indian as a stepping stone between his own exalted sphere and ours." Today he has a devoted internet following, and it's easy to see why. American Indian spirituality is popular, and Silver Birch evinces all that is best in it. On one occasion he was asked how he would explain the "Great Spirit":

> For myself, I would point to the divine artistry of nature's handicraft. I would point to the stars, the diamonds in the sky. I would point to the glory of the sun, to the pale reflection of the moon. I would point to the whispering, murmuring breeze, to the nodding pines. I would point to the trickling stream and to the mighty ocean. I would touch every facet of nature showing how each is controlled by purpose, by law. I would add that where man has made any discovery in the field of natural life, he finds it comes within the orbit of law, that its growth is controlled and regulated, that it is part of one vast, intricate, yet

harmonious pattern, that order reigns supreme throughout the vast universe, controlling planets and insects, storm and breezes, all life, no matter how variegated its expressions may be. . . . "And then I would say, the mind behind all that, the power that sustains it all, the force that controls the whole vast panorama of the universe and many other worlds that you have not yet seen, is what we call the Great Spirit."

Another insight from heaven reaches us from Ambrose Pratt, an Australian who died in 1944. He speaks to us through Raynor Johnson, a psychical researcher turned medium: "Bear in mind above all that God is living, not finished—[not] a static pillar of salt like Lot's wife. He is first and last a Creator, therefore He is creative of Himself, adding to His measure and to eventual bliss all the little souls. Dismiss from your mind the idea of a [changeless] Spiritual Absolute." For Pratt, God's nature is forever being enriched.

After all is said, it might appear that the God of the "lower heavens," where presumably most of us will land soon after our death, is too lofty to be accessible or relevant—we certainly don't meet a deity sitting on a throne surrounded by angels! But in fact our spirit friends have a keener, more lively sense of the Divine than we do. Reading the best of their literature will leave us feeling that the Divine, while awesome and mysterious, is intimately bonded to his (her) creation. A book channeled by Jane Roberts, *Seth Speaks*, took the metaphysical world by storm when it appeared in 1972. "Seth," allegedly an old soul with a long earth history, tells us that God "is not human in your terms at all, nor in your terms is He a personality. Your ideas of personality are too limited." On the other hand,

> He is human, in that He is a portion of each individual; and within the vastness of His experience He holds an "idea-shape" of Himself as human, to which you can relate. He literally was made flesh to dwell among you, for He forms your flesh in that He is responsible for the energy that gives vitality and validity to your private multidimensional self . . . or the soul. [This soul] has then an eternal validity. It is upheld, supported, maintained by the energy, the inconceivable vitality, of All That Is.

He continues, "Such a reality can only be experienced. There are no facts that can be given that can portray with any faithfulness the attributes of All That Is."

Frederic Myers drives home the same point in words that stir the heart. He makes the arresting claim that "God does not love. For love is a human virtue that is like a flame, that leaps up and down." He goes on:

> His fatherhood and motherhood of the Universe never falter, never fail. If He were love, then the marvelous creation of the life you know would have never continued so perfectly. It would have been subject to the changeable character of that thing you call love. At times there might have been cessation of growth—great harvests destroyed, vast tracts of country laid waste. . . . Tides might have spread themselves over half the visible earth . . . many millions of living creatures suddenly perishing. I tell you that if God possessed love, as man understands it, the history of the world would have been wholly changed, changed rather for evil than for good. God is greater than love. That is the phrase you should utter.

The lesson we draw is that the Infinite Source loves in a manner that is absolutely superior to any love we have ever known. We soar aloft in our attempt to imagine what this love must be like. Far from being left out in the cold by a God too abstract for us to relate to, we are profoundly reassured.

This belief in a vast, transcendent, more-than-loving, yet always mysterious Source anchors the religious life of heaven.

5

The Human Self

The spirits have much to say about who we—and they—are. But before we consider their views, let's see what those on earth most qualified to have an opinion on the subject are saying. I have in mind psychologists and philosophers.

For a majority of them the self is "lodged squarely in the field of clinical and research psychology, where it is rigorously defined as a creation of the brain's frontal lobes," as a local psychiatrist put it. The writer is what we call a metaphysical materialist. For him the conscious self is a creation of brain chemistry. The so-called spiritual soul is a fiction, the stuff of superstition, of blind faith. The same with life after death. The same with God. Many materialists don't believe in free will either. We are controlled by whatever happens to our brain, which in turn is determined by our genes, our environment, or both working together.

This is a grim view of human nature, and it's not a scientific position, as materialists like to claim. Most materialists seldom look seriously at evidence that contradicts their dogma. And when they do, it's not to learn what they might from it, but to debunk it. This is not how science is supposed to work. It's how fundamentalism works. It would be a mistake to think that fundamentalists are to be found only among the religious.

It's hardly necessary to point out that spirits, by their very presence, refute this philosophy. All of them left their physical brains behind at death yet still retain all their memories and sense of self. For better or worse, they found themselves thoroughly intact. As will we.

A remarkable spirit communication reached us from England in 1898. Robert James Lees claimed that a spirit named Aphraar materialized himself on a daily basis and dictated the story of his early days on the Other Side. Lees goes on to explain that another spirit, Cynthus, helped him edit the book, and that a third and more evolved spirit, Hyanene, guided the entire process. Lees was obviously a gifted clairvoyant. He conducted séances for Queen Victoria in which the Queen's long deceased husband, Prince Albert, gave her advice on affairs of state. He worked with Scotland Yard on many criminal cases, including Jack the Ripper. And he had the power to permanently heal institutionalized victims of mental illness. He helped found the Salvation Army and befriended Thomas Edison on a lecture tour in America. His accomplishments went far beyond what I have mentioned. I go into his background not only to introduce the present subject of our concern but because we will be hearing much more from him—or rather from the spirits who spoke to him and whose words he faithfully recorded—later in the book.

Lees' spirits are "mind-body dualists"—the soul is one kind of thing, the body another. Spirits tell us that the body, especially the brain, is the soul's instrument. The brain doesn't create or produce consciousness, as materialists claim; the brain receives and transmits consciousness. And when the brain dies, the soul, finding the instrument unworkable, goes elsewhere. In no way is the soul's existence threatened. If anything, it's liberated from its detention in the physical brain. It's free.

Lees' spirits state it this way: ". . . the brain is not the mind, but simply the convenient instrument by which it operates under certain circumstances. Between the two there exists an impassable gulf, so deep and dark that the wisest man has not discovered by what means they are connected."

The spirit of William James might be expected to weigh in on this subject. And he does. A materialist science, he says,

> wants to be free of myth, yet it sets up its own. Only science's myths lack all of those qualities that give men hope, zest, cheer, or faith, by denying not only the meaning of man's universe but of his very own being, reducing his world to a spiritual and psychic vacuum, shoving man out of his own experience and diminishing his sense of stature . . .

Over and over he warns of the perils of materialism, a philosophy he was seduced by for much of his early life on earth and never completely rejected. Until he died. A spirit now, he knows that he is a spiritual being—a soul—who had a physical body before death, and a less dense body now—an astral body. He tells us that the nature of the soul is to be conscious; the soul gives life to the body, not the other way round.

But what is the relation of ourselves to our Source—to God, as we will agree to call Him/Her for the moment? That's a question that gets a lot of print from our spirit friends.

Christian theology has traditionally insisted that God created us all out of nothing (*ex nihilo*). It's hard to imagine a lower pedigree than that. But to see it any other way—to see us as in some way made of the very stuff of the Creator—is an insult to God. At all costs keep the chasm between the Creator and his lowly creatures intact!

But that is not the view of spirits. Silver Birch speaks for many of them when he says that all of us, both on earth and beyond, are "part of the Great Spirit, part of the power which fashioned all life. Man is not so infinitesimal that he is forgotten amidst the vast spaces of the universe. He is always part of the Great Spirit, contributing to the spiritual nature of Infinity." James uses different words to convey the same thought. The Ultimate Source that he experiences as an "atmospheric presence" is uniquely present to itself, but

> so thoroughly does it pervade everything that attempts to isolate it are useless. . . . I *know* that this presence or loving condition forms itself into me, and into all other personalities. . . . Each person is himself or herself, and an agent for the universe at the same time . . . each person is a part of the universal fabric, coming to life.

Betty White, an American woman who died in 1939 and started to communicate shortly after her death, put the same idea somewhat differently. "There is but one reality. It is all-inclusive, but in degrees. Its highest expression on earth is consciousness, the self-aware I-Am of man. Consciousness, in degrees, is the one and only reality." White isn't saying humans are the same as the Source—that would be ridiculous—only that at our core there is something divine-like, our consciousness. We are like God's seedlings. The seedling is not the parent tree, but it shares the same nature. It's as if God, in an act of *noblesse oblige*, deigns to share a part of Himself with us, a tiny sliver of divinity. Imperator said, "We have before us one sole aim . . . we come to demonstrate to man that he is immortal, by virtue of the possession of that soul which is a spark struck off from Deity itself."

This is a far cry from creation out of nothing. It gives a dignity and worth to us that the spirits do not want us to miss. It suggests an intimacy between us and our Divine Parent that would inspire in many of us a happier, more secure, more conscientious way of being in the world.

I could say much more about what the spirits tell us about the human self—us as well as them. But there is space for only the following:

Free will. Zabdiel states the principle simply: "Now, evil is the antithesis of good, but both may be present, as you know, in one person. It is only by free will that that person is held responsible for both good and evil in his heart." A spirit named Stephen who was channeled alongside Betty White said, "Each [of us] builds what we call character. And we know that the extent of the building depends upon the personal initiative of each, on his individual free will." But conditions are different after death for residents of heaven, even the "lowlands of heaven." Drayton Thomas's father explains: "I have freedom of choice. I could do wrong, but I would not. I should not be on that plane if I chose wrong. . . . But we can choose different ways of doing things, just as you have different ways of working on earth. . . . I could not have chosen a wrong way, yet I might have chosen one not so good."

We can relate to this. Mother Teresa could have closed down one of her homes and set up a brothel in its place. But she of course would never have done this in spite of being free to.

Evil souls. Some spirits tend to think that persons are seldom if ever innately bad. James says, "Few men commit an evil act for evil's sake . . . unless they confuse evil with good or justify it as the means to a good end. So in death . . . there are no 'evil' men, and . . . there is no need for mean acts." Others disagree. In 1973 the Rev. Charles Fryer's deceased father told him through automatic writing that God "wills all men to be saved because He made them, and it was out of the overflow of His love that they were made. A very few cannot reach this understanding, and He destroys them without pain or torment because that is all that love can do when it cannot find its return." And Imperator wrote through Stainton Moses that there is a "banded company of adversaries who resist progress and truth, and fight against the dissemination of what advantages humanity." Spirits are closer to the Source than we are, but they are far from omniscient and sometimes disagree among each other.

No hiding what we are. There are no masks in the astral. You can't hide from others what you are: the quality of light shining forth from your body tells all. Mattson tells us that our negative thoughts "go around like big, heavy, sluggish pieces of material – like mud or oil slicks." Even the house a spirit lives in reflects his spiritual stature. These facts can be humiliating at first, but it spurs many spirits on to a greater effort to improve themselves.

Master spirits. There are many descriptions of spiritually advanced beings, usually spirits who have lived in the spheres of heaven for hundreds or thousands of years. Judge Hatch has a hard time finding words to describe a spirit he refers to simply as the Beautiful Being: "Imagine youth immortalized, the fleeting made eternal. Imagine the bloom of a child's face and the eyes of the ages of knowledge. Imagine the brilliancy of a thousand lives concentrated in those eyes, and the smile upon the lips of a love so pure that it asks no answering love from those it smiles upon." A common characteristic of these "master spirits" is the light that shines forth from them; sometimes such a spirit has to dim down his or her natural luster in order not to intimidate. Vale Owen's mother describes such a being: "I could understand, when I thought of it afterwards, why it was necessary for him to condition himself to the lower sphere in which he served. For, as he stood before us now, even though he had not attained the full intensity of his native brightness, yet none of us dared approach him, but drew a little distance away, and left him to stand alone." Are these descriptions of what we can become some distant day? Most spirits declare that this is so.

Most of us are addicted to earth's immediate pleasures and unaware of our hidden depths and destiny. We get a little help from our religious leaders, but we need much more. That's why we should look to the spirits. An unnamed Doctor of Divinity wrote automatically through Drayton Thomas's hand shortly after his passing: "That has been one of the greatest surprises, the feeling that one's life on earth which seemed so important, was only, after all, a period of preparation for the real thing."

6

A Material Universe: Why?

Why did God create a material world like earth, along with all the other planets that almost surely populate the universe? Why not dispense with the grief and suffering that go along with a physical birth, life, and death? Why is all this misery part of the deal?

Many philosophers and even theologians are troubled by what they call the "problem of evil." How can a benevolent and powerful God create a world so filled with scarce resources, mile-wide tornados, malaria and cancer, poisonous snakes, and bad genes? If he really loved us, wouldn't he have wanted to spare us all this? (From here on I'll use the conventional *he* to refer to God—not to indicate gender, but personhood.) And if he was omnipotent, he would have had the power to.

This dilemma has crippled the faith of many thoughtful people. It once crippled mine. But I've come across only one spirit who was troubled much by it. The majority take it in stride as if the answer were obvious. It's in that answer that we find the answer to the question we opened the chapter with: Why did God create a material universe?

The Lutheran theologian A. D. Mattson wrestled with the question throughout his life on earth. Speaking through the medium Margaret Flavell a few months after his death in 1970, he said, "The problem of evil is a very perplexing one. We have not solved it here, either. There is a negative aspect in existence which causes man to react contrary to God's will. What the original source of that negativism is, we do not know—only God knows." But Myers, writing through Cummins, has the beginning of an answer: "The reason . . . for the universe and for all appearances, for even the little mundane joys and sorrows of human beings, is to be found in the term 'evolution of spirit,' the need for complete fulfillment which can be obtained though limitation, through the expression of the spirit in form. For only through that expression can spirit grow . . ." Pratt builds on this theme: "In order to make progress, in order that his self may grow, the religious man . . . has to struggle, suffer pain, perhaps lose faith. . . . There can be no short cuts for him. While he is on earth a certain limitation has to be his lot." One of the many spirits working with Allan Kardec, the founder of Spiritism, put it this way: "Calamities are trials that give you an opportunity to exercise your intelligence, to demonstrate your patience and resignation to higher laws. At the same time they give you the chance to grow in abnegation, selflessness, and love for others." And Frances Banks reminds us of what every spirit says: "The journey itself is compensation enough for the trials of earth."

The quotations above add nothing to the various solutions advanced by earth's best theologians. But no theologian I've read prepared me for this. It comes from Zabdiel:

> . . . the Universe was not created for [Man] alone, any more than the sea was created alone for the use of the sea-animals that dwell therein, or the air for the birds. Man invades both sea and air and calls them his kingdom to conquer and to use. And he is right. . . . But there are greater than he and, as he rules the lesser and uses them for the development of his faculties and personality, so these rule him and use him likewise. And this is just and wise, for these Angels and Archangels and Princes and Powers of God are His servants also, and their development and training are as necessary as that of men.

Zabdiel is saying that even if God could step in and turn earth into a paradise, he wouldn't . For if he did, he would be depriving other spirits, more advanced than we are, of a chance to govern well and grow through their mistakes. God does not manage his planets. He leaves that to advanced spirits. We are confronted with the problems of family and work place—human-size challenges—while they have to surmount problems as big as whole societies or ecosystems. Zabdiel and other advanced spirits like him know we need help in solving our earth-size problems, from racism to global warming. They work unseen on our behalf and in the process grow their souls, just as we do in our much smaller way. (We should bear in mind that someday we may be advanced spirits.)

So why did God, or the Source, or the Creator bring forth so unsatisfactory a planet as earth, a planet that can injure or kill us in any of a thousand ways ? God, say the spirits, designed our world to be a moral gymnasium. We—and they—are souls in training. We work on the planet's surface in our ungainly bodies. They work unseen in their beautiful astral bodies. As one of them put it, when ascending back to her own sphere after a day's work "in the trenches" of earth, some spirits bathe! Their bodies aren't really dirty, but they feel the psychological need to do what they once did after a long day back when they were earth dwellers.

Some athletes prefer to play teams they can beat, but others want stiffer competition. If we are wise, we won't wilt under the pressure of the "stiffer competition" – the rejection by the one we love, the being passed over at work, the tumor — but will fight on. Trusting in the Master Architect, we'll bear in mind that the greater the suffering, the greater the potential for growth. The Great Spirit has given us a world full of physical and moral challenge, and he hopes that we'll use our freedom to choose the good over the bad, to help out when we can, in spite of tremendous temptation to give up. When we triumph in this way we bring value, nobility, and ultimately joy into the universe, and that is what the Creator wants. It's what we, say the spirits, should want too.

7

Progress
Through Stages

Sometimes I ask my students if they think of heaven as a place of blissful rest, a never ending vacation with no more jobs to do or struggles to overcome. Just hanging out with Jesus, or Krishna, or the saints, whoever they might be. Many of them answer yes. "You don't think that might get boring after a few hundred years?" Their brows knit as they think over the question. Others want no part in a static heaven. They want activity, and they have a hunch that heaven is a place of continual growth and that growth requires effort and work.

What do our spirits tell us?

Charles Fryer was a lecturer at an English training college for teachers when, in 1971-72, he developed the gift of automatic writing. After a shaky start his father, Charles Henry Fryer, who had died 40 years before, began to write through him. Charles would hold the pen, and Charles Henry would make it move in a handwriting dissimilar to his son's and at great speed—"at the rate of about three thousand words an hour." Charles Henry explained that he was "one of a group, operating in the 'fourth sphere', that controls me collectively, with [myself] as the actual point of mental contact—a sort of committee of like-minded discarnates who operate in harmony but can act separately." One of the "committee's" most consistent themes deals directly with our subject. Charles Henry wrote on September 5, 1973:

Whereas on the third [lower] sphere we are still very individualised, and have much in common with the life we lived on earth, in the fourth [higher] sphere we enter a sort of common life with others, and share something like a common will and a common source of spiritual energy. You need not suppose my personality is suppressed, however, as it is not like that at all. Rather, there is a vivid intensification of those parts of the personal self which are attuned to the higher life, and a lessening of the parts that are attached to the earth and to lower spheres.

This instruction from heaven makes it clear that spirits can progress. The spirit author has risen from the third to the fourth sphere, so called because it encircles the earth at a greater distance out from the earth than the third.

Furthermore, as Charles Henry states in a later communication, ". . . after some years in this sphere we bear no resemblance to what we were on earth, except that some recognizable traits may persist, such as a tendency in speech, or a strong sense of purpose, or a special fondness for children. . . ." So the progress that spirits are allowed to make is striking, radical, far-reaching. As Silver Birch puts it, we are "pilgrims on an infinite march." And the spirit named Aphraar, after being escorted through heaven's lower glories for only a few weeks, could say, "I could see how occupations were provided to engage my soul through the long eternities which lay before me."

In a later chapter we'll see what these "occupations" are, but for the moment let's be satisfied with a glimpse of the realms where these advanced "pilgrims" live. Aphraar is "overwhelmed with sensations strange and indefinable—not unpleasant, but rather the contrary—I had entered the domain of some invigorating, irresistible happiness, which buoyed me up and carried me forward with an increasing impetus which overpowered and silenced me." He sees before him "countless hills on which . . . terraces were spread—terraces large as plateaus, each [with] mansions, parks, and flowers, like models of angel cities standing in galleries . . ." Yet this isn't the true heaven, but "only a link between the lower and a higher condition of the soul's development." Aphraar adds that he has no idea how many "successive galleries of holiness each soul must climb before it can be satisfied, and see Him [God] as He is." Bewildered and exhausted by more majesty than he can stand, He asks his guide, who was about to take him to a still higher sphere, to take him back in the other direction. Zabdiel, another spirit with a similar message, tells Vale Owen,

> If it were possible that I should take you now into that sphere [where I live] you would not see anything at all, because your condition is not yet fitted to it. What you would see would be a mist of light, more or less intense according to what region of that sphere you were in. In the lower spheres you would see more, but not all, and what you were able to see you would not understand in every part.

It's clear, then, that heaven was never meant to be a static lotus-eating paradise. There are endless opportunities for growth; and growth, as we all know, and as we will see in much greater detail below, requires discipline and self-sacrifice. But the will is free at every level, and no one is forced to take the high road. Zabdiel tells us that spirits eager to rise attend "colleges." He explains that "from the lower to the higher spheres there is a graded system of progress, and every step onward implies an added capacity, not alone of power, but in enjoyment in the using of it."

But not all spirits are eager to rise. Far from it. Judge Hatch tells us through Elsa Barker,

> This is a great place . . . to grow, if one really wants to grow; though few persons take advantage of its possibilities. Most are content to assimilate the experiences they had on earth. It would be depressing to one who did not realize the will is free, to see how souls let slip their opportunities here, even as they did on the moon-guarded planet.

In many respects conditions in the afterworld are similar to conditions here. Many of us on earth, perhaps most, are content to be our ordinary selves, while only a minority are serious about changing ourselves for the better. A former friend once told me, "No one really changes. They just are what they are." I answered back that the whole point of life was to work changes in one's character—to become a better person. According to Hatch, my old friend is not likely to expect more of himself after he dies than he did before. And the heavenly realms will be closed off to him. His destiny, according Hatch and many other spirits, will sooner or later be another shift on earth. But reincarnation is a subject we'll put off until a later chapter.

For now it's enough to say that, according to all the spirits who have communicated their vision to the "moon-guarded planet," heaven is a vital, busy, challenging environment with extraordinary delights—for those who are deserving.

8

Jesus, Christianity, and Earth's Other Religions

How do spirits regard Jesus? Is he coeternal and coequal with the Father, as the Nicene Creed says? Does he live in heaven, and is he accessible? And what of Christianity? Do spirits, looking back, give it first place among earth's religions? Did faith in Jesus give them entry into heaven? Do those who were Christians on earth still think of themselves as Christians? And what about earth's other religions? Do their devotees share heaven with Christians? Or is heaven an exclusively Christian establishment?

From time to time Silver Birch takes a break, a holiday, from the labors of communicating with earth through his medium, the Englishman Maurice Barbanell. He retreats to be with his old friends and equals. He looks forward to tasting "the life [in the heavens] that I knew for so long, that I have willingly abandoned to serve you all [on earth]." These homecomings coincide with our Christmas and Easter, and they are times of great celebration for spirits like Silver Birch. "All the beauties that you have imagined in your greatest moments of inspiration," he says, "pale into unimportance beside the reality that is ours on these occasions."

As Silver Birch continues, we get the first hint of how Jesus is regarded by many of heaven's citizens:

> The greatest joy of all is to make contact once again with the Nazarene [Jesus]—not the Nazarene of the Churches, not the being who has

been misrepresented and exalted and deified into an inaccessible and remote position, but the great human spirit who only seeks to inspire service, who wishes to share his greatness with all who desire to serve his Father and our Father.

We see here that Silver Birch rejects the deification of Jesus while holding him in highest regard.

Judge Hatch refines this idea:

Jesus of Nazareth is a reality. As a spiritual body, as Jesus who dwelt in Galilee, He exists in space and time; as the Christ, the paradigm of the spiritual man, He exists in the hearts of all men and women who awaken that idea in themselves. . . . Jesus is a type of the greatest Master. He is revered in all the heavens. He grasped the Law and dared to live it, to exemplify it. And when He said, 'The Father and I are one,' He pointed the way by which other men may realize mastership in themselves.

Hatch is saying that what Jesus accomplished, so can we.

A number of the spirits who were Christian in their earth lives are critical of the Church and its Christology. Imperator, for example, condemns the teaching that Jesus was sent down by his Father to die for the sins of men in order to gain heaven for us. He has a completely different view of Jesus's mission:

Prematurely was that Divine Life cut short by human ignorance and malignity. Little do men grasp the significance of the truth . . . when they say that Christ came into the world to die for it. He did so come: but . . . the drama of Calvary [and death on the cross to atone for our sins] was of man's, not God's devising. It was not the eternal purpose of God that Jesus should die when the work of the Christ was just commencing. That was man's work, foul, evil, accursed.

Another description of the relationship of God to Jesus is attempted by Drayton Thomas's father, John. Drayton asks, "Does God bear the same relation to worlds in the farthest part of the universe as He does to this world?" John answers:

Yes, He is the Supreme and Only Being. The question must have come to some minds, "Are there different Gods in the different systems of worlds?" No, only one God. But there may be, from what I have heard, in each system and possibly for each planet, some holy one of His creating who is Master and Saviour of that system.

John, a Christian minister in earth life, of course has Jesus in mind as the Master and Savior of our planet.

A spirit giving his name as John Wesley, the 18th century founder of Methodist Christianity, allotted to Jesus a somewhat humbler station. Speaking through the celebrated American trance medium Cora Richmond, he maintained that Christ was to his own age what other teachers both before and after him had been to theirs. "These cyclic visitations of truth" come periodically in earth's history, he claimed, in accordance with God's "infinite law."

You might have noticed that most of the spirits we've looked at were Christians during their earth life. The reason is that a majority of otherworld accounts available in English came from Christians—after all, most of the population of Europe and North America until very recently were Christian. China has long been fascinated by the nature of the afterlife, but their "morality books," produced by Chinese spirits speaking through Chinese mediums, have not been translated—though a few have been briefly summarized. The Native American Black Elk shares a vision he had of the afterlife, but it, too, is short and undeveloped. We can be sure, however, that Jesus gets no mention in any of these books. Finally, a well developed vision of the afterlife comes to us from Paramahansa Yogananda, who acted as medium for his deceased Hindu master, Sri Yukteswar. He tells us that Jesus had achieved his final freedom but chose to come back to earth "as a prophet to bring other human beings back to God." And that's all Yukteswar says, just the briefest of mentions. I have no doubt that we are getting a somewhat skewed account of Jesus' place in the total scheme of things. I think we can safely say what he means for many Christians who have died and "gone to heaven." But we have no right to say what he means to non-Christians.

As far as I can tell, many devout Christians upon dying have been introduced to a new way of seeing Jesus. On the other hand, he is real and accessible and very much in the hearts and minds of those who loved him on earth. Some spirits are impressed by his humility. Eight weeks after her death Drayton Thomas's aunt told him she didn't "see Him upon a throne. I did not see Him crowned. But I saw Him! And he seemed to stand there simply, very simply, and as a friend." Finally, we see from all these accounts that opinions among spirits vary. No one can safely claim the final truth about Jesus. Some of the richest spirit accounts don't even mention him. Spirits are no more God than we are. They are not omniscient.

We're now in a position to evaluate Christianity in the context of the world's great religions. Where does it stand according to spirit accounts?

A few Christian spirits claim first place for Christianity, but not on theological grounds. For example, Betty White said, "Of all the faiths that have lived, Christianity has done most for the world; in envisioning individual and collective liberty, in belief in the self, democracy, education, real freedom." Drayton Thomas' father said, "There are many good Buddhists, Mohammedans and others who, at first, are satisfied with their own conception of the highest, whether as Buddha, Mohammed, or other, as the case may be. The idea of Jesus Christ does not at first appeal to them, but later it does." That's because, as W. T. Stead put it, they realize "that the teachings of Christ were of the highest. Always He spoke of Love as the binding link and the force of all good."

But nowhere are non-Christians singled out for damnation or even second-rate status. The young Texan Leslie Stringfellow experienced the afterworld as a place of travel and adventure. On one of his "foreign trips" he and several other young companions explored the spirit worlds occupied by "Turks and Hindus" and on another trip the Chinese. Muslims, he tells us, "have some of the finest cities you can conceive of and in one there is a temple which excels in outward splendor anything I ever saw. . . . It was what you would call a mosque." He adds, "Some seem to think that the spirit world we enter immediately after death has but a single religious form, but this is not so." He next describes his trip to astral India.

> Well, darling mamma, here we are. Have just been on a trip to the Spirit World that lies over the Hindu Empire. . . . We went to a city called Delphi [he means Delhi] where there are some of the oldest temples. . . . Of course their conception of God is very different from ours, and they keep their same notions when they first come here. . . . After a time we went to another place more modern that bears the name of Calcutta. There it was all a scene of life and gaiety, and everybody seemed to be enjoying music, painting, sculpture and art.

44

Quite an upgrade from the earthly Calcutta! But a description that most educated Indians would recognize as authentic—Calcutta is India's culture capital.

About China the young adventurer says, "I believe these are the grandest gardens I have seen, because they are on such a grand scale. These gardens have thousands of tall pointed summer houses, and crowds of visitors go in and sit and chat." About their music he was less complimentary: "Of all the hideous groaning and growling and creaking, you never heard the like. And just to show how people's tastes differ, I looked around after the overture was concluded, and the whole crowd were in a broad grin of delight and were applauding for all they were worth." He leaves us with the following observation: "In fact, I believe every nation, when its people first pass over, keep the same characteristics that marked them on earth."

As we saw in Chapter 3, there are numerous sectors in the afterworld, spread out geographically as on a map. And all indications are that no one is necessarily disadvantaged by growing up in a non-Christian or non-Western culture or race. But is there never a coming together, a joining of cultures and races, a transcending of all those things that work so much mischief on earth? Spirits make it clear that people tend to retain their looks, and that includes color and other racial features. But these recede in importance among those who advance upward rather than downward. Theologian A. D. Mattson says,

> We are all walking. We Christians walk here, the Hindus walk there, the Buddhists walk in another place, and so forth. All have their own paradise, goals, aims, and objectives for so long. Then suddenly they are into the tremendous experience of knowing that all is one under God and that there is no division in purpose.

Vale Owen's guide, Zabdiel, describes an event in which 300 "old Persians" turn their backs on a treasured altar where sacrifices to their fire god were performed: ". . . they decided to leave that Altar behind them, and to go onward themselves into the wider Brotherhood of God's Household of the Heavens."

It's not just non-Christians who must outgrow their old religion. The Anglican nun Frances Banks, speaking to us through her old friend Helen Greaves, says, "Unless we can break out of the prison of old-fashioned expressions, creeds and formulae, we shall never be free to find the far more glorious truths which are inherent in the Christian religion."

What are those truths? Aphaar, in his quaint old Victorian prose, puts it spot on: "We recognize but one religion here, that is—Love; and all its disciples have but one denomination—lovers of mankind. No one of all the man-made religions holds a monopoly of this attribute. But earnest and conscientious followers of it may be found in all."

This pluralist vision is given a cosmic dimension by Vale Owen's mother. In a spectacular statement she tells her son:

> At times . . . earth and earth's affairs retreat into the background, and glimpses are had of what eternity and infinity mean. . . . Then it is seen that the whole Church on earth is but a small portion of the Divine Kingdom, which includes . . . not only all races and all systems of religion here below, but also that realm of interstellar glories and powers the mere contemplation of which the human heart grows faint and the reaches of human imagination fade into the boundless infinities pulsating with the heart-love of the One Ineffable Light.

It's worth repeating that many spirits have no interest in the subject of this chapter. As we saw in the previous chapter, just as great numbers of earth-dwellers are indifferent to the life of the spirit, so it is in the afterworld. The advanced spirit known as Imperator makes this point: "Many of those who are withdrawn from earth are not, as you know, very progressive, nor, on the contrary, very developed. The majority of those who pass from the body are neither very evil nor very good in spirit." In the chapters that follow we'll look at what happens to such persons in the afterlife.

9

Judgment

In Chapter 2 we saw that earth's two largest religions, Christianity and Islam, picture every soul going through some sort of judgment following death. Most Christians believe in two distinct judgments, one immediately following death, the other when the world ends and all men and women who have ever lived are publicly judged. Islam teaches a similar double judgment. The traditional reward in both faiths for good and faithful souls is eternity in heaven, while the punishment for wicked or disbelieving souls is eternity in hell.

What do the spirits say about judgment? Do we get away with our misdeeds, or do they condemn us to hell? Does saintly behavior merit a special place in heaven, or do we all end up in the same happy place? Does good or bad character have any impact on the quality of life in the hereafter? Most of us are constantly playing the blame game—the media sees to it! Is this habit of passing judgment on everything that happens around us, and *in* us, a petty planetary pastime, or does it go to the very heart of who we are? Are we programmed to make judgments? Is it the inevitable outcome of free will? Is it one of the most important things we do? Is it something that God does?

Judgment is a central concern, not only of spirits newly dead, but much further along. Let's begin with those who have recently passed. "When coming to this land," says W.T. Stead, the Titanic victim, "that whole record [of one's thoughts and actions] has to be dealt with. Not by a judge in wig and gown, but by our own spirit selves. In spirit life we have a full and clear remembrance of all these things and, according to the quality of these individual thoughts, so we are brought into a state of regret, happiness or unhappiness, despair or satisfaction." Drayton Thomas' aunt told him that

> The Judgment to come consists in being able to see ourselves as we are, and by no stretch of the imagination being able to avoid seeing it. It is a judgment of God on us through our higher selves.... and no other person could be so severe or just a judge of us as we ourselves can be when facing the truth. For many it is a terrible hour.

We get a vivid picture of this kind of suffering in the following statement, made by an elderly unnamed woman two years after her death:

> I have had the most disturbing experiences. I don't really know how I lived through them.... One of the tasks set me was that of looking back. I have been shown the effects of all my acts upon other people's minds. Their thoughts were shown to me. It was the most awful and humiliating experience.... I have seen what is called "the emotional reactions" to my own acts.... On the whole, I deserved what I got.... I am changed. I am a much softer person now.

A spirit calling himself John Worth Edmonds, a New York Supreme Court judge and influential 19th-century Spiritualist, gave a moving account of his judgment. He had died 19 months earlier and spoke through the same Cora Richmond we met earlier—spoke in front of a large audience while she was in trance:

> And all my life, every thought and deed came up before me, as though it was a personality. Every false opinion; every harsh word and judgment; every person to whom I had breathed a word of unkindness, or of whom I had thought unkindly, seemed to stand before me in my mind's vision condemning me. I saw my faults and my imperfections like realities. Pride, with its lofty head; uncharitableness, with its finger of scorn— all these in procession. Then I despaired being raised into the sphere of my companion and friends and became desolate.

> Then there seemed to come from the shadows around me, persons to whom I had extended, in my official capacity, the leniency that was rather born of justice than of charity; some upon whom I had perhaps bestowed alms; others whom I had aided to overcome earthly difficulties, and each of these came around me with some offering of

48

peace or of love, some flower or token of remembrance; and as they came, the shadows seemed to fall from my eyes, and my raiment grew brighter. Then I saw criminals for whom I had secured pardon, and on whose account I had been unjustly censured upon earth. These came with their offerings, and they, more than all the others, seemed to shed brightness upon my pathway. But chiefly the crowning conquest was to forget the injustice that I supposed I had suffered from any human being when in the midst of my earthly life, and to cast aside the hatred and unjust thoughts I had held toward such. Then, in that instant of spiritual existence I felt that I could rise to another state.

A. D. Mattson tells us that few people on earth have any idea how significant their ordinary acts are. They don't suspect, therefore, that these acts, or failures to act, will have consequences in the world to come. Mattson wants us to see they do:

When any individual, on earth or here, omits doing something that he feels and knows he should do, the whole creation feels that loss. Whereas when we do something that adds grandeur and stature to life, the whole created universe gains from that action. It can make you shiver to know and appreciate how far-reaching a thought or deed or word of any person can be.

Another judgment account comes to us from Frances Banks. In life she had been a highly respected teacher, a licensed psychologist, a nun for 25 years, and "an earnest seeker after the spiritual life." But, like the rest of us, she made mistakes. She was said to have had a "will of iron" and could be "obstinate and obdurate." A month and a half after her death in 1965, she reported she was shocked to discover she had gone into flesh with a blueprint, a plan she and her guides had worked out and that she intended to carry out in her new life. Placing this blueprint next to the actual life she lived, she saw they "differed exceedingly." You find, she explained, "that you did so little when you would have done so much; that you went wrong so often when you were sure that you were right."

Her whole life was spread out before her, and she saw it "in a kaleidoscope of pictures." But there was no one judging her, no God on a throne. Instead, "You are the accused, the judge, and the jury."

Where there is judgment, reward or punishment must follow. And it does—just as much in the world to come as in ours. The main difference is that in their world justice is perfect, whereas in ours it seldom is and therefore carries overtones of harshness. This harshness needs softening; we call it mercy. But mercy has no place in the afterworld. Aphraar explains: "You have been in the habit of thinking of justice as necessarily allied to oppression. It is so on earth, but you will not find that here; therefore you have to learn that with us it means strict rightness, and if you add mercy to that on behalf of either party, the adulteration produces injustice."

Justice isn't a one-time affair either. The first judgment, Imperator tells us, is complete when, shortly after death, the spirit "gravitates to the home which it has made for itself. There can be no error. It is placed by the eternal law of fitness." But later on, perhaps much later, "the spirit is fitted to pass to a higher sphere, when the same process is repeated, and so on and on until the purgatorial spheres of work are done with, and the soul passes within the inner heaven of contemplation. . . . Judgment is ceaseless, for the soul is ever fitting itself for its change."

We learn the following from these spirit accounts. First, we are the judges of ourselves, and our memory of everything we did is extremely acute and cannot be evaded. In 1977 William James reported, long after his death in 1910, "I can experience any season of my life in an expanded fashion, using heightened memory that actively creates events, giving me awareness of an event as I once experienced it—but expanded to include all of those personal details that escaped me at the time." Second, although the world's major religions are correct in telling us we'll be judged, they are wrong on the details—seriously wrong. Nowhere is there mention of a God sitting on a throne with scepter in hand. Nowhere does it seem that some external being of any kind does the judging. God may well be the ultimate judge, but if so, then, as Drayton Thomas's aunt tells it, he does it "through our higher selves." Third, judgment serves a single purpose: the reconstruction of the soul. The process will often be painful, but the goal is never punishment, but change. Fourth, the idea of eternal hell is universally rejected. At every level, from angelic to demonic, the will is always free, and therefore change possible. No one is condemned to remain in hell even for a season, much less everlastingly.

10

The Law of Karma:
A Woman in Hell

According to our spirit friends, our deeds, especially when they have congealed into habit by repetition, dictate our fate after death. The law doesn't work mechanically in tit-for-tat fashion, with Hitler having to live 6 million abject lifetimes to atone for every Jew he killed. The hating character he became in the process of authorizing all those murders is what condemns him. Drayton Thomas's sister, Etta, nicely captures the psychology of this law as it pertains to life after death:

> When one is fitted only for a low plane, no amount of desire to be on a higher or more beautiful one would suffice to take one there. The habit of life on earth decides, and not any chance desire. If a man has qualified for a lower sphere, he will find himself there, and he cannot get away from it [until he begins the arduous process of change]. That is just and right, and it saves a vast amount of supervision. According as the soul moulds itself while in the body, so it decides the place to which it must go on leaving the body. Those who simply live in the physical senses find themselves exceedingly limited on leaving the earth. We wish such people understood the facts, so that they might realize how fatally unwise and shortsighted is their manner of life.

In what follows we'll see how the law of karma works itself out in actual lifetimes.

Leslie Stringfellow, the Texan who died at 20, was an only child deeply loved by both parents. Free of personal corruption, he helped his father develop a 2,000-acre pear orchard near Galveston. His mother, a pianist, taught Leslie the violin, and from a young age they participated, often together, in the local "music circle." She was devastated by his death after a three-day bout of malaria. In desperation she looked for some means of making connection with him and eventually found a local medium who taught her how to use a planchette. More than 4,000 messages came from him over a 14-year period.

Many spirit accounts shine with amazement and joy over what is discovered after death. Leslie's is typical of this genre. He tells his mother,

> I am so happy, dear Mamma, to see that you and Father realize that I am indeed with you and that nothing you could have done for me on earth would have given me the happiness I enjoy here. I am safe and as happy as I can be. . . . Never doubt for a moment that this world is a thousand times better in every way than yours.

A similar message comes from Etta Thomas. She tells her brother that "the four years since I passed over have gone very quickly and very happily. I grow more conscious of the wonderful things around me, things of which I was not wholly conscious at first. For instance, my range of sight and hearing, as well as my understanding, is constantly increasing." Two years later she told him, "Nothing I could say through this channel would give you an adequate idea of its reality. It is so much more wonderful, bright and enjoyable than we can express."

But, as we saw in the previous chapter, happiness is earned. Suffering in the afterworld, not just joy, can be intense; it exists to awaken the soul to its errors so it will long for the happiness of those higher spheres, where corruption can't enter. We'll explore those heavens— those places where love reigns unchecked. But for now let's see what happens when it doesn't.

In all the afterlife literature I've read, I've never come across a story as rich in detail or feeling as that of an American woman named Marie who lived and died in the late 19th century. She shows us what a life lived badly leads to. The word "retribution" jumps to mind.

She tells her story to Aphraar, who passes it on to the medium James Lees. Lees reports it in ornate Victorian prose, and I'm going to translate it here and there into more modern English for better effect. Here is a study of the way karma really works—not by decree of some high god or cosmic jury, but by an inner force growing out of one's moral history.

I am an American, the only child of a Southern millionaire, idolized by my parents, pampered, proud, and willful from my infancy. When I wished for anything I only had to speak and it was mine. My education taught me that money was almighty, and as its supply to us was practically unlimited, I grew up with the idea that I was to be obeyed, and no wish I cherished or expressed could ever be thwarted. Of course this tended to make me very exacting—even overbearing—but I was by no means cruel or wicked as the world would judge. Having the money, I had the right to all the pleasure it would bring, and if my enjoyment was unfortunately the cause of pain to another, I was not to be blamed for that; it was their misfortune, and they had no right to expect me to forego my desire out of consideration for their feelings. Such was my philosophy, and I acted upon it.

We were church people, my father always liberally contributing to the various agencies promoted by it; we were faithful in our attendance at the services, and my name was duly enrolled as a member when I reached the appointed age. Whenever I felt inclined or desired an excuse for breaking an irksome engagement, I would give the excuse of going to Sunday school or paying a "charitable visit." . . .

There was only one girl I could really call my friend—that was Sadie Norton. Our social position was fairly equal, but since I was a little older, I rightfully assumed the premier place. Then Sadie wasn't exactly the girl to command or lead anyway, so I was in no way interfered with when I took the lead, and for that reason our friendship became very close. A friendly rivalry existing between our parents was to some extent reflected in us, but without lessening the sisterly feeling which had developed; if anything it strengthened as the years passed. We were always together, and no festival, social, home gathering, or surprise party was considered complete unless we were there. On every project put forward at the church we were consulted. Every philanthropic cause sought our patronage. And before we were out of our teens every eligible boy in the town and country was angling to catch us. This fact led to a great increase in our fun. Not that we ever thought for a moment about marrying, but we seriously interfered with many other girls who did want to marry, and for a year or two we got a kick out of the number of matches we were able to break off.

Then one day a fine young fellow came along, bringing very satisfactory credentials to my father and others, and all the girls in the town set their traps to catch him. Sadie and I decided to go for him as well, and by playing him, first me then her, keep him from anyone else, as well as give him a hard time. But he took matters in a most serious light, and before a month had passed made me a formal proposal. I must confess that I too felt very serious about him and would have accepted him if it wouldn't have ended the game that Sadie and I had promised to enjoy together. So I laughed at him, and when he enlisted my mother's aid, I stood on my dignity and very cavalierly told him I was not of the marrying kind. He went away looking very crestfallen, but I only laughed.

My experience of men had not been a long one, but I was sure his cloud would only last till sunrise. Every man enters upon the April season of his life when he falls in love, and the way he is treated and trained by the woman he woos has much to do with the formation of his permanent character. So I thought, and therefore I decided to give him a schooling that would bring out the hero in him—someone I could trust my keeping to, at least as far as I thought prudent. I made a mistake. The next day passed but brought no Charlie. I was dismayed. He was trying to master me, but he would find his match in me. A week passed but I did not see him. Neither did Sadie, for I had prepared her in case he should try to flirt with her. A month went by without a sign of him; circumstances had also prevented me from seeing much of Sadie. Then we met. It was at her birthday party, and the first thing she told me was that Charlie had proposed. My face lit up at the thought of the fun we were going to have. She continued— and told me she had accepted him. The blood rushed back to my heart—I stood speechless as a statue. In a moment my blood boiled and dashed through my veins in cataracts of maddened fury. Jealousy and disappointed love devoured me; my brain reeled under the strain; I fell and remember no more.

The day they were married I was swinging in the balances of life and death from brain fever. All through my delirium their names were seldom off my tongue, pleading, entreating, or cursing them as the frenzy drove me; but after my reason returned I had the strength of mind never to mention them again. The magic potion of wealth was pressed into service in every conceivable form to wean my thoughts from my sorrow, and so skillfully did I play the part in the early days of convalescence that everyone was relieved that my condition wasn't as serious as first imagined. Little did they dream that my composure was only a mask and that in my soul I was plotting and planning how best to get revenge, which I would either succeed at or die trying. Sadie had been false, had taken advantage of our temporary estrangement to carry out her base design, and she had succeeded with fatal effect. She had deceived Charlie as wickedly as she had injured me, for it was impossible she could be the wife I should have made him. He was not so much to blame since he had only been the tool of her cunning duplicity. But she would feel the full weight of my vengeance. I would find them if I had to travel the world; I would return her betrayal fourfold and take him from her even if I died in the hour of my triumph.

For five years I continued my secret but unsuccessful inquiries, but never for one moment faltered or forgot my vow. I so perfectly hid my jealousy that my acquaintances began to think I was really happy again. How little we know of the real man while we rapturously applaud the actor! The stage and the home often have a gulf between them just as closed off from each other as Lazarus and the rich man. And we poor simpering fools laugh at the actor's memorized lines but have no insight into his true character. I was deaf and blind to everything except the one object of my life. Everybody thought I was happy while in fact nothing on earth or in heaven could make me so but the man I had lost, and who had been stolen from me by my ungrateful seeming friend.

By accident I discovered where he was—from a small paragraph in an old newspaper I was cutting a pattern out of. I saw his name, learned all that was necessary, and immediately began formulating a plan for reaching him. Life from that moment brought me hope, but my excitement almost ruined everything. Now I wish to God it had! Anyway, having found him, it was easy to go to him since an old college friend was living in the same town, and arranging to pay her a visit took only a matter of days. My next step was more difficult since everything depended on our first meeting.

One rash or false move and all would be lost. But even her fortune—
or, as I now know, misfortune—favored me. I met him accidentally,
and alone. He recognized me and spoke before I was aware of his
presence. I saw his agitation, knew his old love was not dead, and
by an almost superhuman effort preserved a seemingly indifferent
calmness even when I asked about his wife. I read volumes in his reply.
He had discovered his mistake, was not happy, and the assurance of it
made me frantic with delight. He was mine—I knew it—if only I acted
with caution, kept my hand concealed, and waited for the appropriate
opportunity. We met several times in the same way, but he never once
visited me where I was staying or invited me to his house. It wasn't
long before he asked me to keep a clandestine appointment. I refused.
He urged it for the sake of "auld lang syne." Finally I gave in. From that
point on I was lost, but that was the price I had calculated to pay if I
could win him, and I had done it. In less than a month he deserted
his wife and children, and we were hurrying away east.

I was happy now that I had repaid Sadie's deceit in her own coin. I
could never be Charlie's wife, but that was nothing. I was his, he was
mine, and my account with my rival was square. We were together
and alone, and that was all I had craved for. My prayer for revenge had
been answered. In my rebellion God stood aside and let me gather
all the necessities for a heaven of my own design, and when the work
was finished he invited me to enter. Then, lo! I found my heaven to be
God's exquisite and perfect hell.

Having accomplished my desire, and the tension under which I had
lived so long now being over, a speedy collapse followed. I had never
fully recovered from my first illness, but my craving for revenge had
given me strength that came at the expense of my overall constitution.
As soon as I had gotten my wish and the need for treachery was over,
the tax on my vitality put in its claim, and it was clear that I had only
a short future before me. In less than two years I was a confirmed
invalid, unable to move, and we were forced to face the awful fact
that I was dying. At this time my father found me. H reproached me
for the dishonor I had brought upon his name and vowed that if ever
Charlie crossed his path he would shoot him like a dog. I pleaded with
him, but he was determined. He told me Charlie had left me just as he
had left his wife. He had disappeared from the town and gone no one
knew where and that it was impossible I could ever see him again. All

the old fury came back at this, followed by brain fever, then delirium, and finally a blank. [At this point Marie has died, but, as you will see, she is unaware of it.]

When I awoke it was dark, horribly dark. I could almost touch the blackness, and I was lying on a bare floor, cold as a block of ice. I called Charlie—my father—my nurse! But there was no response except the echo of my own voice, which seemed to mock and rejoice at the terror I felt creeping over me. Where was I? Great God! Was it possible I had gone mad, or that I had been placed under restraint to keep me from following Charlie? I rose to inspect where I was, to see my surroundings, but in the fever of my fear I fell—fell without the strength to rise. All my senses resolved themselves into the power of feeling—quickened and intensified a hundredfold so that I might contemplate with horror the process of my own petrification—voiceless, sightless, sleepless.

How I prayed for the fever and delirium to return and conquer the icy terror that crept so slowly, so agonizingly over me. Vain prayer! I was a prisoner in the frigid domain of despair, beyond the reach of help, or rest, or pity; the playful toy of all the remorseless machinations that accompany such a state. I was slowly converted into a block of frozen—yet living—flesh, and my abnormal sense of feeling heightened as the infernal transformation went on. Why was it? Where was I? Who were my relentless persecutors? How long before the morning would break? Would the day bring me relief, or wake me from the agonizing dream? These and a thousand other queries piled up their unending enigmas for my additional punishment, till I would have gladly rushed into the arms of madness for rest. But alas! I was deprived of even that consolation. Eventually my feet, my hands, my head, my eyes, my tongue, my heart, my brain were icebound. Then the furies boiled in my blood and sent it in maddened cataracts through my veins to top off the excruciating pain, which I could only suffer while lying motionless.

When all that ended I have no recollection. Whether I suffered until the pain wore itself out from its own excesses, or whether the intensity of my torture became an anesthetic and lulled me to sleep remains a mystery. All I know is that for a while my existence lay in oblivion, but of its duration and nature I can't say.

When my memory again took up the thread of life I was still in the state of semi-palpable darkness amid a silence that terrified me to listen to. But the sharp agony of my suffering was over—or rather, I should say, a respite had been granted while a new torment even greater than the first was being hatched. I still didn't know where I was. I didn't understand the nature of the great change that had taken place. But I was quite conscious I had gained strength, was free from actual pain, and had acquired the power to move if I wanted to. I also recognized how greatly my condition had improved from where I had been before I lost consciousness, but I yearned for some degree of light, either natural or artificial, so I could make out my surroundings and make some guess as to what had taken place.

The duration of this suspense, in which my only companions were the fantastic shadows of the subterranean gloom, was too long for me to appraise. It seemed to be centuries, but I know now that wasn't so. At length—oh! such a length—I had my wish partly granted. I saw a light; but it was so small and far away that it was useless for my purpose. As soon as I saw it I became conscious of an involuntary movement, as if I were being irresistibly drawn in its direction. At first I experienced an almost imperceptible gliding sensation gradually increasing in velocity until I was lifted off my feet and borne rushing through space as if on the wings of a hurricane. On and on. League after league, with an ever increasing momentum towards that magnetic beacon of light that, expanding while I traveled, yet appeared to be as far away as ever.

Oh! the fear and suspense with which that aerial voyage filled me! It was not the pain of my previous punishment, but the dread of the consequences that might be waiting for me, that weighed on me now. Suddenly the power which had carried me along seemed to be exhausted, and I fell, scared but unhurt, on the threshold of that light. It radiated around the only person I sighed, and wept, and groaned for. It was Charlie! I had found him, was with him again. Something told me that the force that had carried me here—reluctantly in my ignorance—was connected by some means to his intense desire to see me; and in my new-found happiness at our reunion I wept and reproached myself for the hard thoughts I had entertained against the unknown benefactor who had come to my relief, released me from my prison house, and brought us together again in spite of my father's opposition and strategy.

Then something new dashed my hopes by suggesting that what I saw was only a hallucination—the cruel vagaries of a dream, and that I would wake up to find my father as unbending as ever, and Charlie gone I knew not where. The thought of this was unbearable, and the shadow of such a suspicion could not be allowed. I decided to take measures at once and remove the doubt.

I passed into the circle of light that enveloped him. How greatly he had changed since we parted. His jet black hair was lined with silver, the once calm face was furrowed, the brightness of his eyes was dimmed, and his strong upright body was bowed. At the moment he was thinking of me, and I was conscious of his passing through an ordeal almost as fierce as mine. As I reached his side he murmured my name. His hand moved as if to take mine; but lost in the depth of his reverie, perhaps unsuspecting that I was near, he didn't raise his eyes to meet my hungry gaze, which was feasting on his presence. Oh! how happy I felt. His tone and manner told me he loved me as much as ever and made me afraid to carry forth with my plan.

He hadn't returned to Sadie, but driven from my side had found his retreat—where it was I didn't know or care—where he had perfected a plan for my deliverance. At least that's what I thought. He appeared to be lost in abstraction as he nervously awaited the result—so lost that he didn't realize he had me right in front of him and had achieved the result he sought. I lifted my head and saw that the faraway look had not faded from his eyes, where I noticed a strangely suspicious light was beaming. I started to my feet in horror and tried to shake him, afraid that the joy of our reunion had proved too much and that his reason had deserted him. He only shivered as if the room had grown chilly. Then I questioned my own sanity. Could it be possible my mysterious journey had been the delirium of a mad woman's craving? "O! God!" I cried, "remove this mystery or it will kill me. Charlie, Charlie! Don't you know me? Speak only one word, and tell me so. I've been ill, but I've never swerved in my love for you. If you think I've done wrong, oh! my love, forgive me, and let me nurse you back again to health. We will be happy yet. Come, let's go away. Say you know me and I'll be content. Charlie! Just one word, dear; say you know me!"

At this he roused himself abruptly, picked up a book, and began to read without so much as a word, a look, a sign that he saw me. I recoiled in amazement, dumbfounded. He wasn't angry, but how could I account for this unwarrantable treatment? Why wouldn't he speak? Surely if my presence was unwelcome he would tell me so. [Charlie can't see her because she has no physical body; she has descended for the moment to earth. If Charlie were clairvoyant, he would see her as a ghost. Marie doesn't know yet that she has died.] If he thought I might be discovered, he would do what was necessary to conceal me. If I was still the same to him as before, he would clasp me in his arms and greet me. I couldn't account for my reception, unless I was the victim of a dream. God knows my suffering was real; it was no dream! But what else was real? I could only wait and watch. After a while I scolded him for his conduct to see if I could get a response. But he only smiled, wearily laid his book aside, turned to someone [a child] I couldn't see, and said, "Will you tell your mamma I want to speak to her?"

What did he mean? What was any other woman to him when I was present? Was it possible he had gone back to Sadie after all and wished her to be at hand to witness my humiliation? All my old jealousy was aroused at the thought, and a sudden frenzy carried me past all restraint in anticipation of the coming scene. I felt a stranger enter but couldn't see or hear who it was, a fact adding to the mystery and terror that possessed me. Was I equally invisible and inaudible to her? It seemed so, for while I heard every word Charlie spoke, and saw every movement he made, and could understand that the conversation made no reference to myself, I was ignored as completely as if I had had no existence.

Was it possible they were playing an arranged part to drive me to distraction? Who was this woman? Oh, God! that I had been equally deaf and blind to Charlie's conduct as she was to me. It was not Sadie, but I heard him call her by a name he never could have given to me. Then I understood his baseness and treachery and found a full explanation of the conduct I had received. He was simply mocking me. Whether she was aware of my nearness or not, he was aware of it. [Marie is of course mistaken in this assumption.] He had brought me here so I might witness his happiness with a rival who had supplanted me, as I had taken him from Sadie—that he might laugh as he saw how the knowledge of it would torture me. This was too much. The certainty of his desertion maddened me; but to witness his love passages with a rival goaded me into a diabolical frenzy, and I made up my mind to kill him before her eyes. Alas! Before I had time to move, the light that surrounded him expired, and I was left again in that Egyptian blackness, afraid to stir because of the terror that came along with my blindness.

Still I could hear him—worse, I could hear her; heard, without the power to stop my ears, or prevent my knowledge of what she said and called him. Rage and jealousy tormented and mocked my helplessness, until I prepared to follow the sound and wreak my vengeance by laying them dead side by side. Horror! As soon as I made up my mind to kill them, I found I was as powerless to move as to see, and I had no choice but to stand and listen to his monstrous behavior, unable to make a sound to drown out the echoes of his caresses.

A thousand times over I would have chosen the earlier state over this one. The tortures of hell were increasing. Was it possible there could be anything even more excruciating? I prayed to go mad so that in my madness I might find relief from my pain, but my prayer came back like a stream of molten lead falling on my head and burning fiery channels into my brain, increasing my agony even more, and making me aware that my retribution was just beginning, that it would get worse, and I would have to bear it since no escape was possible. I was chained to him; and for periods of time, as long as eternity it seemed, I was made to endure this indescribable chastisement, with every nerve quickened to a degree defying description, while memory itself is not strong enough to recall its intensity at the time. Madness could not come to my relief; death could not listen to my pleadings; unconsciousness was out of the question; pity was beyond the reach of my wailing; and mercy had no power to enter the place where I was prisoner.

What could I do? Nothing but suffer! Why could no one wake me from such a horrible nightmare? I cried, but there was no one to answer me. I was in all the agonies of hell without the poor consolation that I was suffering in company. I could not bear it; yet I could not escape. Was there no possible limit to human endurance—no high water mark of vengeance which, having been reached, would serve as atonement for my sin? I had to get help from somewhere—anywhere—so long as it broke the infernal monotony of my ever increasing pain.

I had such a keen and lively sense of the tortures accumulating around me that I would have gladly served with slavish obedience any power that would change my condition if only to vary the punishment. If change were out of the question, I would make a last appeal: "Oh, God or devil! Any being of pity or remorseless cruelty, hear me, and end my torments! Take me, tear me, or destroy me. Drown my reason past all hope of restitution or, by one tornadic blast of torture, put an end to feeling and terminate this agony. Hell! Hell! In mercy take pity on my condition; open your gates and let me bathe my sufferings in your fiery lake. Hell! Hell! I say, in mercy open and let me in!"

So ends Marie's extraordinary story. We've seen how spoiled a child she was, how superior she felt to most of her peers, how she delighted in breaking hearts. Then, when she doesn't get her way, she is devoured by jealousy and devotes the rest of her life to avenging Sadie's "crime." She breaks up Sadie's marriage to Charlie and seduces him to run away with her and leave his children behind—all without a twinge of conscience. Marie is bad to a degree that few of us are. Her character is deformed and misshapen. If she can be salvaged after she dies, then there is hope for just about everyone.

One of the most surprising discoveries you'll make when studying spirit literature is how confused many of the dead are about their condition. Marie is such a spirit. She shed her earth body years earlier but doesn't realize she died. Therefore, when she enters the light that contains Charlie, she can't understand why he doesn't see her. She thinks he's play-acting in order to torture her. But of course Charlie really doesn't see her. He's not making love to his new girl friend in order to punish her; he has no idea she's looking on. Marie's torture isn't inflicted by Charlie or God or the Devil. It's self-inflicted. Karma isn't a juridical process working itself out in order to punish; it's a psychological process designed to correct—a process that arises from the depths of one's own soul and can be excruciating.

Aphraar tells us that at the end of her narrative she fell exhausted at his feet and that twenty earth years had passed since her death. He cries out to his spirit guide, an advanced spirit named Cushna, "Twenty years! Oh! What a hell! What an Experience! How I wish she could preach such a sermon to the ears of earth!" Cushna then tells Aphraar she has told her story many times:

Marie has now reached the healing stage, and every time she tells her story it is like another dressing of her wound—painful for the present, but beneficial in the result. Every recital is less agonising than the last, and the exhaustion it causes induces a sleep from which she derives additional strength, which is necessary to her progress.

The story of Marie would not be complete if I failed to mention that she is constantly attended by a heaven-based spirit named Azena whose sisterly devotion is designed to love Marie back to health. Such heroic devotion is at the core of heaven's everyday life, as we'll see in a later chapter.

Another example of the way retribution, or the law of karma, plays itself out in the afterlife of a spiritual shipwreck will help fill out the picture. It's taken from Frances Banks' narration. In Chapter 3 we were introduced to the Shadowlands, and that's where the action takes place. You'll recall Frances was an Anglican nun for 25 years before her death, and she is now living with fellow nuns who have passed. As nuns ideally do on earth, they do in the afterworld: they enjoy bringing healing to troubled souls. She begins by describing the setting:

> Mother Florence, two other sisters, and I made our journey into what you would call the Underworld. Here we prefer the description Shadow Land, for this is indeed a Land of Shadows. The journey to this place is difficult and wearying, for we have, by concentrated thought power, to "slow down" our vibrations so that our [astral] bodies will be enabled to endure the physical conditions pertaining therein. The Sisters never go without the special Messengers who guide them there and conduct them to the various stations on the way.

She describes a meeting with a depraved soul—what we might call today a "low-life"—who had been a painter living in Paris. After his death in a knife fight, he finds himself in a ghetto with fellow boozers and drug addicts. He continues to paint, for what else does he know how to do with his time? His many paintings, which he stores in a dirty, smelly hovel, are dark and ugly, but each has a closed door with a thin streak of light outlining the door as if to suggest there is light on the other side. With this hint, Frances gathers hope and tells him there is a way out of his hell. "There are places here," she says, "where painters like yourself live and paint the natural beauties of the countryside." He doesn't believe her, though, and tells her he's heard this "old story" before. Over and over he insults and curses her. But she persists.

"You *know* such places?" he finally asks with a sneer.

"I know them."

But he's still not convinced. He tells her he doesn't have a permit to get to such a place and lacks the oils to paint light even if it existed.

Mother Florence has by now arrived on the scene and tells him she can arrange passage if he's willing—it completely depends on him. She asks a male helper to get the oils, and after more reassurances, the painter dares to hope. "Hunching his shoulders in a gesture of astonishment at these strange happenings," he walks with the helper "towards a hill where the gloom was threaded with a spear of brightness."

Our painter friend is another wrecked soul—whether more damaged than Marie we can't be sure. It's noteworthy that he was brought to his dingy neighborhood shortly after his death by a process not described, but his livelihood from that point on is entirely self-imposed. No gate pens him in, and no judge has imposed a sentence of so many years and days. We see that help is given him and that he's disinclined to take it. Only because Frances and Mother Florence persist so doggedly does he let himself hope. What becomes of him we aren't told. But one thing is clear. In Aphraar's words, all suffering is "probationary and remedial." And it's never everlasting.

Another case will make it still clearer that the suffering of a spirit arises naturally from the spirit's character. Judge Hatch describes a group of spirits who were alcoholics before their deaths:

What do you fancy they were doing? Repenting their sins? Not at all. They were hovering around those places on earth where fumes of alcohol, and the heavier fumes of those who overindulge in alcohol, make sickening the atmosphere.... A young [living] man ... was leaning on the bar, drinking a glass of some soul-destroying compound. And close to him, taller than he and bending over him, with its repulsive, bloated, ghastly face pressed close to his, as if to smell his whiskey-tainted breath, was one of the most horrible astral beings ... I have seen in this world since I came out [died].... The hands of the creature were clutching the young man's form, one long and naked arm was around his shoulders, the other around his hips. It was literally sucking the liquor-soaked life of its victim, absorbing him, using him, in the successful attempt to enjoy vicariously the passion which death had intensified.

But was that a creature in hell? You ask. Yes, for I could look into its mind and see its sufferings.... this creature was doomed to crave and crave and never to be satisfied.

And the young man who leaned on the bar in that gilded palace of gin was filled with a nameless horror and sought to leave the place; but the arms of the thing that was now his master clutched him tighter and tighter, the sodden, vaporous cheek was pressed closer to his, the desire of the vampire creature aroused an answering desire in its victim, and the young man demanded another glass.

This man is what we call these days an "earthbound spirit," and there number is apparently legion. Zabdiel describes them:

It matters not whether they be clothed with material bodies, or have shed them and stand discarnate; these are bound and chained to the world, and cannot rise into the spheres of light, but have their conversation among those who move in the dim regions about the planet's surface. These, then, are holden of the earth, and are actually within the circumference of the earth sphere.

In a way these cases are even more unfortunate than those of Marie and the painter. It's hard to imagine a more pathetic and humiliating situation than that of the earthbound spirit trying to navigate a physical planet without a physical body. They are like birds without wings or fish without gills. Yet we meet them everywhere in the literature of spirits. Addiction to drugs or alcohol while on earth is bad enough, but what it does to the addicted spirit is even worse. Over and over the spirits tell us that our habits don't disappear with death; they follow us into the grave, then emerge intact on the Other Side.

How different is the fate of Aphraar, a decent but undistinguished man on earth whose mother died when he was born; a man never married and childless. He died in the act of trying to save a child—both were trampled by horses. A few weeks following his death he was being led to a house that was to be his. He describes the scene (rendered into modern English):

Others were constantly joining us. Some brought instruments, others had wreathed themselves in flowers. My guide and I gradually became the central objects in a long procession, joyful and exultant as they sang their songs.

Presently we entered a narrow valley between two ranges of hills, then ascended a gentle slope until we reached its summit. There below us was a city magnificent beyond any earthly comparison. . . . Everything, everywhere, as far as the eye could reach, spoke of wealth and wellbeing. As I looked over the wide area of the city, I asked myself if it was possible I should find my home in such a happy place.

As we paused to survey the scene before us, a chime of bells added their welcome to the music that surrounded us. . . . It was at this moment that I realized all this ovation was for me, but I could scarcely believe it until I turned to my guide and asked,

"Is this really for me?"

"Yes, my brother!" he replied, "in this city you will find your home for the present, and our friends have come to welcome you." . . .

I wish I could find words to convey even a faint idea of the beauty and completeness of the house. . . . Jesus Christ, speaking of the many mansions in His Father's house, said to his disciples, "I go to prepare a place for you." But what about the house's furniture? This is a thought that had never entered my mind until I entered the house. What a revelation! Every piece of furniture, ornament, or decoration grew out of some act, word, or feature of my life on earth. What a stunning, rather frightening discovery! . . .

One of the rooms contained a series of pictures. . . . In every case the original design of the picture, perfectly visible, was slightly spoiled in the execution. Putting them side by side I could easily make out the weaknesses in my character that needed correcting before I could advance to the next level. In studying them I could estimate the work that lay before me. . . .

My guide led me past one doorway over which the curtains were closely drawn. A silent voice seemed to be calling me to enter, but my guide led me up to the roof, where I could take another view of the city. The interest that this view aroused overcame the agitation I felt when passing the forbidden door. . . .

When we again reached the door on the way back in, he waved his hand for me to enter alone, then went on and was gone. . . .

In that room there was someone waiting to welcome me home . . . one who had sacrificed her life in giving me mine. . . . If she had lived for just a few years, so that her memory could have remained with me, how different my life might have been. . . . Now I ask you to pardon me while I pass through the draperies, and for the first time in my whole existence as far as I know to look upon that long-sought face . . . the face of my mother.

Aphraar was no saint—he begins his account by describing himself as something of a misanthrope—but he had a big heart for London's paupers and befriended many of them; some of these made up the party that welcomed him to his new home. In his own view he was "recompensed" for his service to them with the house that kept no secrets from him, a house he felt unworthy of. Finding his mother was, of course, the ultimate reward—at least for the moment.

But reward and punishment don't reside only in external things. They are found in one's very appearance, and that's the most sobering fact of all. To the extent that we are vain, and we all are to one degree or another, we will recoil at the following report by Zabdiel:

So those whose radiance is great go into those spheres whose brightness agrees with their own; and every one into the sphere which agrees with his—be it less or more. But those whose bodies—spiritual bodies I mean—are of gross texture, and do not radiate much light, but are dim, go into those dim spheres where only they may be so much at ease that they may work out their own salvation. They are not at ease indeed in any sense of the word; but they would be less at ease in a brighter sphere than in those dim regions until they have grown in brightness themselves.

It's like having a debt you can't pay. The last person you want to bump into at a party is your banker. But if you have an account flush with cash, you can have a jovial chat with him.

What about deathbed "conversions"? Spirits tell us they are meaningless. That's because they have no impact on character. Judge Hatch has a warning for those planning on such a maneuver to gain them admittance into heaven: "Beware of deathbed repentance and its after-harvest of morbid memories. It is better to go into eternity with one's karmic burdens bravely carried upon the back, rather than to slink through the back door of hell in the stockinged-feet of a sorry cowardice." Silver Birch echoes Hatch: "There is no cheap reprieve, there are no easy pardons. Divine justice rules the whole universe. A spiritual dwarf cannot pretend to be a spiritual giant. There is no deathbed repentance."

What about the rich and famous, the pampered and adored? Will their fan base carry them into heaven? Not a chance. Monsignor Benson explains:

> However mighty we were upon the earth-plane, it is spiritual worth only that takes us to our right place in the spirit world, and it is the deeds of our life, regardless of social position, that at our transition will assign to us our proper abode. Position is forgotten ... deeds and thoughts are the witnesses for or against us...

What about ordinary people who gamble away their paychecks in Las Vegas or commit adultery with their best friend's spouse or curse like a sailor on the golf course? What about ordinary selfish people who might remind us of ourselves? A spirit describing himself as a politician who "got the most out of people and gave the least possible in return" told Drayton Thomas about his first surroundings. He likened them to

> some of the dull, uninteresting towns in the Midlands or North of England with their stretches of barren fields around small rows of jerry-built houses. My companions were uninteresting and unintelligent people. Many of these had been wealthy on earth, but it is not that which counts on coming over here.

This man eventually aspires to a better state:

> On reaching the next sphere my surroundings were a degree better, for there were opportunities for more intellectual and spiritual development. There I found halls and schools where study was encouraged, and helpers came who did not coerce, but who told us of the more beautiful regions above. Yet, although they can tell of those

realms, and can arouse the wish to reach them, one has to work out the stupidities and follies and the errors of evil done, whether consciously or unconsciously, during life on earth. And this is accomplished by hard work for others, while forgetting self entirely; building houses and making the less beautiful objects required there, aiding those newly arrived, and, generally, in effacing self while recollecting one's truest needs.

In this chapter I've concentrated for the most part on hellish and heavenly states, but this man's realm is in between. We could call it a kind of purgatory. Perhaps it is the state that most of us will land in soon after we die.

11

Suicide

S uicide is an act that usually carries with it a grim entrance into the next world and is universally frowned on in spirit literature. Why is this? The answer surprised me when I first read it, but it now seems obvious.

Medium Maurice Barbanell asked his spirit guide Silver Birch, "Did the Great Spirit intend that some human beings should 'die' before they fulfilled their plan of life?" Silver Birch answered:

> The plan is always that you should enjoy a full expression of earth so that you shall be equipped for the greater life of the spirit. . . . If fruit drops from the tree before it is ripe it is sour. All life that is forced to quit its body before it has achieved its maturity on earth is unprepared for the world of spirit.

Premature quitting of the body includes much more than suicide, of course. Accidents, fatal diseases, war casualties, and starvation are tragedies, but they aren't within one's control; they aren't self-inflicted. But suicide is by definition self-inflicted and is always within one's control. The spirit of Betty White told her husband that suicides break a solemn law because they deprive their conscious selves of a natural growth that life in a physical body can best provide. She says:

> . . . the more quantity [physical experience] one attains in the obstructed universe [of a physical planet], the more beautifully he will be able to go on in the unobstructed universe [of spirit]. Indeed, just that

accumulation of quantity is the reason a long life is desirable. That is why we have to look on suicide as cowardice. The suicide is the fellow who is not willing to accumulate as much as possible.

But it's not always that simple. The motives for suicide vary greatly; many factors are at work in determining conditions in the afterworld. In certain conditions euthanasia, for example, might be acceptable; and the motive behind the death of a desperately unhappy adolescent would be completely different from that of a Wall Street financier jumping out of a window following a stock market crash. Motive dictates conditions. And whatever the conditions, help is always available. Spirits are well aware of all these complicating issues.

We're going to look at three examples of suicide to learn how spirits look upon them. The first reaches us from the spirit of Mrs. Coombe-Tennant by way of the famed medium Geraldine Cummins. The spirit is telling her son about a friend of hers named Eveleen and her son, L., both of whom are presently (in 1957) with her in the afterworld:

> She [Eveleen] has now in this [spirit] life slowly and painfully realized how much she injured L. in his early years through her possessive love for him. It has indeed been her purgatory to see how much she contributed to the ruin of his life on earth, and how unhappy were the consequences for him after his death. His suicide led to his being plunged into darkness and isolation here for a very long time. L. had as well inherited the instability of abnormal possessiveness from his mother. It was not expressed in the desire for property, money, but in other ways and in a self-centredness. But I cannot go into those details now. It is sufficient to say that your Aunt Eveleen's possessive love even led her subtly to antagonize the boy L. against his father. His father was idealistic, devoted to spiritual things, so L., disliking his father largely through his mother's jealous influence, became a materialist when he was a man. Later in life he developed a passion for a very beautiful married woman, who also was spiritually minded and of course rejected his passionate possessive love. All this—her spirituality, his father's spirituality, failure to possess this woman, drove him to unbelief and gave him a tortured mind. Eventually he took to drugs and, as you know, killed himself. . . . He took into this life [of spirit] his crude ego that hated and hated and [his experience of] denied love. So he suffered much. Poor Eveleen sometime after coming here had to perceive, as we all have to, the consequences resulting from

her life on earth. She saw how much she was responsible for her son's ruined life on earth. She has been very brave about it and, though her reception by L. was grim, she sought him out and tried to help him out of his hell of her and his creation. She has done much to improve things for him.

Note the quality of L's retribution. He was "plunged into darkness and isolation for a very long time."

Now compare his fate to the next case, which reaches us from Imperator speaking through the medium Rev. Stainton Moses in 1873. Moses asks Imperator how his "friend," a suicide, is getting on in the afterworld. Imperator, I should tell you, is never one to sugar-coat the truth. Perhaps he speaks more harshly than necessary.

He begins by telling Moses that his friend's "spiritual state is low." "Is he unhappy?" asks Moses. Imperator replies:

How should he be blest? He lifted sacrilegious hands against the shrine in which the All-Wise had placed his spirit for its progress and development. He wasted opportunities and destroyed, so far as he was able, the temple in which dwelt the Divine spark, which was his portion. He sent forth his spirit alone and friendless into a strange world where no place was yet prepared for it. He impiously flew in the face of the Great Father. How should he be blest? Impious, disobedient, willful in his death, heedless, idle, selfish in his life, and yet more selfish in bringing pain and sorrow on his earthly friends by his untimely death—how should he find rest? . . . The fostered self-hood dominates him, and makes him ill at ease. Selfish in his life, selfish in his earthly end, he is selfish still. Miserable, blind, and undeveloped, there is no rest for such as he till repentance has had its place, and remorse leads to regeneration.

The medium then asks Imperator if there is any hope for his friend. "Yes; there is hope. Already there stirs within him the consciousness of sin. He sees dimly through the spiritual gloom how foolish and how wicked was his life. He begins to wake to some faint knowledge of his desolation, and to strive for light."

In both this and the previous case, "selfishness" and "self-centredness" are crucial factors in their decision to end physical life. Imperator calls selfishness "the plague-spot of the spirit, that which wrecks more souls than you dream of. It is the very paralysis of the soul." But in both cases help is available and gladly offered. However, recovery is usually slow. "Characters are not so easily changed," Imperator says, and seldom does "the fire of purification work so rapidly." Imperator then tells Moses to "pray for strength to minister to him." The spirit of AD Mattson, the Lutheran theologian speaking through the medium Margaret Flavell, also encourages prayer. Suicides, he says, "are greatly helped by the prayers and supportive thoughts from those still on earth. They are also aided by those [spirits] from the higher planes who are dedicated to help them grow spiritually."

We might get the impression from these two cases that suicide almost always leads to grave and extended suffering. According to Jon Klimo, a specialist who has studied the fates of suicides in the afterworld, not all suicides face a future so grim. Some, he tells us, "can pass through [the lower] astral plane so quickly that they do not even really notice it." The spirit known as Seth adds that there are no "special 'places' or situations or conditions set apart after physical death" that the suicide has to experience. He elaborates:

> I mention this here because many philosophies teach that suicides are met by a sort of special, almost vindictive fate, and such is not the case. However, if a person kills himself, believing that the act will annihilate his consciousness forever, then this false idea may severely impede his progress, for it will be further intensified by guilt.

For the rest of this chapter we'll be looking at the case of an adolescent boy who took his life but escaped the extremes of gloom and self-torture we've just beheld. His story will show us, at the very least, that there isn't a single rule that covers all cases.

"This is a book about the life, suicide, and afterlife of my son, Stephen. He took his own life when he was fifteen years, three months, and fifteen days old, because he felt it hurt more to live than to die." Thus begins Stephen's remarkable story, partly narrated by his mother, Anne Puryear, and partly by Stephen himself from the Other Side. Puryear, a medium, tells us she received the message by dictation, but only after many months of futile waiting while sitting with notepad in hand or in front of her typewriter. Eventually her patience paid off. "I would hear a voice inside my head, talking to me. . . . I spoke to him out loud; he usually spoke to me telepathically. Occasionally, he spoke out loud so clearly that I turned in the direction of the voice." Later she adds, "I could hear the words inside my head—words that I wasn't forming or thinking, that moved my own thoughts aside." For several years before Stephen began his dictation she had been listening to her "spirit guides," and they spoke to her in the same way as Stephen. Nevertheless, at the beginning she battled "doubt and skepticism" over the source of the voice. Sometimes Stephen tried to convince her he was real by recalling to her some event from his life. Finally, and decisively, she could no longer doubt.

Those of you who worry that Puryear might have imagined in her distress the communicating presence of her son should bear in mind that Stephen has been dead for quite a few years before he begins communicating the rich and detailed narrative you are about to read. He took his life in 1974; her book was published in 1992. Hysteria as the explanation of the voice is out of the question. Moreover, Puryear is a gifted spiritual counselor who co-founded, with her husband, the Logos Center in Phoenix, Arizona. She lectures widely (I've heard her) and is considered an expert on teen suicide. She is someone we can trust.

Also, bear in mind that Stephen is no longer a fifteen-year-old boy when we hear from him. He has died, lives as a spirit, and has been in school "every day." His teachers have a wisdom that we know little of. It's time to turn over the narrative to him. He is always speaking directly to his mother, often in answer to a question:

> What you need to hear next is about suicide and what happens to those who kill themselves. . . . The day I died, here's what was happening. Remember, I see it now from a clearer perspective than when it happened. . . . I was in a depressed state from the wrong diet, loneliness, and being uprooted from my schools and friends. I was depressed because I didn't feel I was worth much. No matter what I did all my life, I could never please Dad. I felt guilty for skipping school. You know how much I had always loved school and the teachers and my friends. Now I hated it every day. . . .

> Mom, you just weren't enough then. You were busy. You were my mother. Part of being my age and growing up was to pull away a little anyway, to become a little independent. . . . I just knew that how much you loved me and how good-looking you thought I was didn't mean much. I actually thought that you loved me no matter how fat I was and wouldn't tell me how awful I really looked. . . .

> I turned right around and didn't go to school when you let me off. I sneaked back home. I ate and watched TV and felt worse and worse.

I decided not to be humiliated more. I would be gone when you got home. I decided to go to the woods and spend the night where you couldn't talk to me. I might even kill myself. . . .

I had brought a rope along, not to hang myself especially, but I always brought a rope camping. Remember, Dad taught us that. So I began to plan and practice certain knots with it. Then I wrote a few things, then I would think. I climbed up the tree. It was getting late in the afternoon, dusk, almost time to start getting dark. I sat on the limb and let the rope down to touch the ground, then shortened it so that my body wouldn't touch the ground when I jumped. I might jump and hit the ground if it weren't just right. So I climbed up on a higher limb. That ought to work for sure. I knotted the rope around the tree limb, so it wouldn't come undone. Then I put the other end around my neck with a perfect slip knot. . . .

I was scared then and started to cry . . . I'm sitting there with the rope around my neck, wanting to be stopped, and yet not wanting to be a coward by backing out. I don't think at the time I had any thought that someone might come and find me. . . . I was pretty far back in the woods and nothing could have stopped me then. . . .

First I was going to jump. I stood up. It looked so far down, it scared me. I started crying. So I sat down. I kept trying to make myself do it and couldn't. Then I forced myself and jumped. Not a real jump, just a kind of slide and easing-myself-over-the-limb jump. I died instantly. I did feel a moment of pain. I'm not going o tell you I didn't. There was a moment of blinding pain. The pain only lasted for a little bit and it stopped.

I felt like I was floating up. I was like an air bubble under the water. It felt like I had dived into deep water and was coming up, but I could breathe in the water. I floated up out of my body and it felt like there was somebody at each elbow, but I couldn't see anybody. And I looked around and there were kind of misty-like forms, but I couldn't see them very clearly. I floated above my body. I looked down. I could see the top of a head, and then I kind of floated away and could see this body hanging there by the neck. For a moment I couldn't figure out who it was. It didn't look familiar.

When I realized it was me, panic took over. I mean *panic*. Instead of being excited that I was out of my body and was still alive and could see and think, I suddenly realized how mad you and Tom were going to be. I had this moment of feeling like a kid that had done some bad thing and was going to be caught and punished for it. I didn't realize that there was no way you could punish me for this. I had created my own punishment. I started to really cry; tears filled my eyes and I sobbed. I hurt so bad, and my heart was pounding—I felt like I still had a body. I felt just like I always did, except that I wasn't touching the ground. I was suspended in the air somehow, without falling.

And as I looked around, the forms around me began to become clearer. I saw grandfather H. I didn't even remember him except from his pictures, and there he was. I saw your grandfathers. I saw a lot of people that I'd only seen pictures of in the albums. I saw a couple of friends of mine—not real friends, but acquaintances that I had known, and I remembered that they were dead. I saw a whole lot of people I didn't know, but I felt like I knew them from somewhere. I was confused and didn't know what to think. I was sad, but I was also surprised, and I was kind of excited. I guess I stopped crying. Some of them came up to me and hugged me. Others said, "Hi, Steve." All I could see were the people. I felt so much better. Then when I looked, I could see the body hanging there. It gave me a terrible feeling each time I saw it. It grossed me out. I didn't want to look at it. It was strange. I knew it was my body, but it didn't look like my body. I had my body, it seemed. It was confusing.

Panic set in again. Then this cold feeling all over. Maybe I was going to throw up. Then I began to feel I was going to sleep. I just felt myself moving upward and away. Kind of a swishing sound. I just moved upward and away and I fell asleep. There was a lady there helping me, a sweet and kind lady dressed in white, who held my hand.

The next thing I knew, I woke up and it was daylight, and I felt so good. I just felt wonderful. I looked around and there was kind of a misty look everywhere, then it got clearer. I looked closer. I was lying down on my bed, and there was a window. I could see the sun outside. And I tried to remember where I was. You know how you wake up in a strange room or someplace and you don't know where you are? I couldn't remember where I was. I had some vague thought come to me that I had seen somebody hanging in a tree, and I fell back asleep. . . .

I kept waking up and getting afraid and then very gently going back to sleep. Someone came and sat by me. I could hear them talking to me, then I'd go back to sleep. . . .

Mom, I know this isn't easy. I know how it hurts and how sad it makes you. Just kind of breathe deeply and relax. I remember waking up again and this really nice lady was sitting beside me. I thought at first she was a nurse. She had on a white dress. Just a sweet, nice lady. She didn't say her name, but she talked to me quite awhile. I felt like I knew her. She said, "Would you like to go for a few minutes and see your mother? She has just been told what happened to you. She's hurting a lot." And I said, "Yeah, how do we get there?" She said, "Just come with me," and she took my hand and it seemed like the next time I was in the living room standing beside her as you sat on the couch, and two men sat across from you.

I was so shocked, I didn't say anything for a second, and then I said, "Mom, Mom! It's me, Steve. Mom! You won't believe what happened!" You didn't answer me. You didn't even look over. I thought you were too busy talking to them to see me. I didn't want to interrupt you, so I saw Tom and said, "What's wrong, Tom? Tom, what's wrong?" He didn't look at me or answer either. I looked around. There were Andrea and Debbie, and Tom's kids. I turned to Andrea and said, "What's wrong, Andrea?" She was crying and she didn't answer me either. The woman very gently put her arm around me and said, "They can't see you. They can't hear you. But we brought you here to see your mother and be with her."

I said, "Am I dead? I am dead, aren't I?" And she said, "That's what they would say." I said, "Oh, NO!" Suddenly I felt so embarrassed to be there, because I felt that you and Tom could see me, and how irritated and angry you must be. Then somehow, even though you weren't crying, I could feel your hurting inside, your heart inside my heart. I had never hurt so bad, ever. Not even when I jumped from the tree.

Then I remembered again the pain and jumping off the tree. It had been like standing by a cold pool and dreading jumping in the cold water. Thinking I had to, then doing it and feeling the shock of the cold water when I hit. Then the pain stops and you get used to the water. Only this pain wasn't stopping. I wished I could go back and not jump. I must have been crazy. . . .

I felt sick. I wished I could kill myself to stop hurting. Funny statement, huh? Here I am "dead" and wishing I could kill myself. Not so funny in this dimension, by the way. No matter how much you hurt or how bad you feel, you can't kill yourself here. I hated what I had done to you. I never realized how much I loved you and you loved me. I never realized how much I loved my home and the girls and Bob. I wanted to be back. I screamed at you, "Mom! Mom! I'm here! I'm here, Mom! Look! I'm not dead! I'm *here!*" . . .

I hurt so bad. I forgot that no one could even hear me. The lady could, though, and said, "Steve, let's go now." I said, "No! I want to stay." . . .

The lady asked me again if I was ready to leave. I didn't want to go. I said, "Where is my body? I want to see my body." She nodded and I followed her. There was something on a stretcher. Tom came out and they pulled the cover down and there I was. Yuk. It grossed me out. I looked awful. My hair was all messed up and my skin was strange looking. It didn't look like me at all. I didn't want anyone to see me looking like that. Suddenly I had a thought! What if I jumped back into my body and then I couldn't be dead? I would just sit up and walk into the house and say, "Fooled you, I'm alive."

I tried it. I went over and tried to squeeze into my body, but I kept slipping out. I finally made it but nothing happened. I could see and hear just like I was in it, and I could sit up, but the body didn't move. I tried and tried. I tried pulling my hand up, getting under my shoulders and pushing myself up. I couldn't budge the body. I couldn't even lift my own hand.

I turned around and said, "Help me." The men in the ambulance didn't hear me but the lady did. "Please help me get back in my body," I begged her. "I can't do that," she said. . . . Steve, you can't undo what you've done. You can't use this body anymore. There is nothing I can do. There is nothing *you* can do here. Come with me and we'll get you settled and talk about all this." . . .

"Why are you here?" [he asked her]. Are you an angel? If you aren't an angel, then why are you here? Are you dead?"

"I guess people would say I'm dead," she laughed, "But don't I look alive? You will discover that dead doesn't mean what you have always thought. And I'm here because my job is to help young people like yourself, who come here to visit a little too early, get adjusted and acquainted. I am not an angel, but there are angels here." . . .

I looked around and it wasn't all that different from where we lived except that it wasn't familiar. There were trees and birds and streets and houses and people everywhere. Some were friendly and happy, some spoke to us, some walked by without speaking, others waved. There were kids my age and every age, playing and running and walking with their friends. There were some old people, but not many. . . .

I was miserable. I tried to act happy, but there were things I needed to take care of back home. This was not where I was supposed to be and I knew it, even if the lady didn't, and I was going to find some way to get back. . . .

I followed you. You grabbed a shirt of mine on the bed and tucked it under your face and cried and cried. I held you, but I still couldn't really feel you and you couldn't feel me, and that made me crazy. I really was dead. Dead. Dead was supposed to be *dead*. I could hear and see and do everything I had ever done. I was not really dead. I knew I wasn't, but everyone else thought I was. What could I do? This was awful. You were crying because you thought I was dead. I'm hugging you and trying to tell you I'm not, and you don't even know it.

I am explaining all this to you, Mom, because it's important to understand the unbelievable pain and frustration I felt. . . .

It was a very difficult time for me. Back in my new room, I asked to go see Dad and the lady said, "Let's wait a bit. Let me take you somewhere." We walked down the hall of this house where my room was until we came to a big building. We entered a large room, like a library. There were tables and people sitting around reading and looking at things. . . . I spotted a book on life after death. When I picked it up, it had a funny feeling to it, like little electrical things on my hand. I opened it, and as I looked at the words, I could read them and feel them go inside my head. It was the strangest feeling, like the words would become pictures in my head. I could read and see and hear at the same time. The book was about the changes when you died and how you need to prepare yourself for what it's like not to have a body. At the time, I thought it was a strange coincidence to find that specific book. Now I know it was part of what I had to learn if I were to grow. It was no coincidence at all." . . .

As I got to know the lady who helped me over and took such loving care of me, I found out a lot about her. She was a mother. All her own children had been killed in a fire, and then her husband left her before she died. On this side, she was able to reconnect with her children and then, out of the agony she had experienced, volunteered to be trained to help young people like myself. Her role wasn't just to meet me when I died. As I began to make choices which could end in a suicide, she was assigned to me to try and help me choose differently [well before I died]. She did all she could, but I was beyond listening. She was there to help me once I made the final decision. I know you will think this strange, but I never called her by name nor asked her name. I didn't need to.

One of the reasons I waited so long to help you get this book out was that you weren't ready to bring it through with all this information. We wanted you to feel very sure it would discourage, not encourage, anyone to take their life. Plus the world wasn't quite ready for it—it is now. I needed time to prepare. You needed time to grow and get out of the relationship with Tom. And you needed time to heal.

Stephen provides much more detail about his life on the Other Side than there is space to tell here. The full account can be found in his mother's book *Stephen Lives!* I think three points need to be underscored. First, Stephen feels a seering regret for what he's done; he is fully aware that he's made a mistake, and that feeling will stay with him for a very long time. While disclosing to his mother all the disappointments that led him to the "crazy" deed, he never tries to excuse himself. He wishes he could undo the deed. Second, neither hell nor heaven awaits him. Instead, a motherly spirit tries to guide him step by step. She becomes his first otherworldly mentor. He was, after all, a child. The grim harvest that awaited the adult suicides we looked at earlier would not have suited Stephen.

We see him suffering profoundly, but not unjustly. Third, he tells us that spirits hovered around him as he gave up the body. Not just the "sweet lady," but others too. And they continued to guide and teach him once the deed was done. In other words, we see expressions of love for the suicide in the world of spirit. And Stephen becomes in time a teacher in his own right. His mission is to serve those of us on earth who might be tempted to a folly similar to his. He too is motivated by love.

As we will see in the next chapter, loving service is the highest calling of the religious life in the afterworld.

12

Love and
Service

By now we've become accustomed to seeing life in heaven as
a long process of spiritual growth. A common mistake that
Christians and Muslims make, according to all spirit communicators, is to suppose that God intervenes and takes us into his
presence, where we bask for all eternity in blissful repose. They tell
us that even for the supposed saint the process is in its infancy. Much
more is expected of us, and those of us who answer the call will rise
to heights undreamed of in earth's theologies. "Answering the call"
is the religion of heaven. No one is required to practice this religion,
but the wise will see its beauty and grandeur, even its necessity. And
their rise will be proportionate to their labor. Their labor will sometimes bring them exhilarating joy, at other times disappointment
and even sadness. Heaven isn't unbroken bliss. Heaven is the world
where spirits who practice this way of life live. Revealing its nature
and its attraction—not only to spirits but to many of you—is the purpose of this chapter.

First let's see what heaven is *not*. Imperator tells Christians their
afterlife is "no sensuous ease in a heaven of eternal rest; no fabled
psalm-singing around the great white throne, whereon sits the God;
no listless, dreamy idleness, cheaply gained by cries for pity, or by fan-
cied faith; none of these . . ." Charles Fryer's father was surprised when
he learned this:

When a year or so had passed of your time we began to look together at the question of what I was to do. . . . You can see my difficulty: I was not prepared for work or effort, and had incorrectly thought that eternity was a place of endless rest, but this is certainly not the case; there is work to be done in our life which is as important as what is done in yours, and we are given a choice as far as possible.

So what *is* the "religion" of heaven? What is the nature of the "call" that needs to be answered? Drayton Thomas puts it concisely: "The ruling principle is service to others, and sharing happiness." AD Mattson tells us that "God still gives us the opportunity and responsibility in the spiritual world . . . to serve." Frances Banks tells us that she desires to advance "to a sphere for which my whole soul yearns" and that the key to progress is "continued service." Serving, doing something useful, benefiting others—heaven vibrates to this kind of music. But service, after all, can be a joyless grind. The kind of service described in practically all spirit sources, however, is rewarding, even when it isn't well received, even when its rejection brings pain to the one serving. That's because the service is lit up by love. And love always carries joy in its wake. Imperator says, "We have our work still to do; and in doing it we find our delight."

In heaven there are innumerable ways to serve; we'll be looking at some of them below, but first let's hear what heaven's residents say about love. "Everywhere we go," says W. T. Stead, "we are conscious of the general love for one another. It is much more evident than on earth, and that great affection is the direct cause of the general brightness and radiance of this world." But this love doesn't just shine outward to other residents of heaven; it shines downward. Silver Birch says, "Remember, I am not only a teacher, seeking to teach eternal truths and reveal the powers of the spirit: I am also the friend of each of you, for I love you dearly and strive always to help you with all the strength and power that I possess." There it is, service lit up by love, but this time love for us. Nowhere is the primacy of love brought out more forcefully than in the following instruction given Aphraar by an advanced spirit: "Love! This life in all its phases, its multiform developments, its heights and depths, is but a grand commentary on that one word. Love is the only study we pursue—the food we eat, the life we live." But love doesn't come easily to heaven's residents. It must be worked at, perfected. Advancement depends on such mastery. Zabdiel explains:

This is one of those things which make for difficulty in this life of the spheres. For not until a man has learned to love all without hating any is he able to progress in this land where love means light, and those who do not love move in dim places where they lose their way, and often become so dull in mind and heart that their perception of the truth is as vague as that of outward things.

There are, on the other [hand], mansions here which sparkle with light in every stone, and send forth radiance over the country round to a great distance by reason of the high purity in love of those who dwell in them.

A few examples will show how seriously this religion of love is taken and how difficult it is to master. Saintly Ambrose Pratt yearned to experience mystically the Divine during earth life, and this yearning carried over into death. There were moments when heaven's glory filled his soul to bursting. But, he tells his friend Raynor Johnson, "Such experiences are only granted me when I have earned them by hard and sometimes painful work—work for creation which sometimes leads me into a region of shadows—work among the little souls of a lower primitive order." We've met a few of those little souls in earlier chapters. Marie is a good example. In Chapter 10 we left this "poor, wounded, crushed soul" in a faint following the terrible agony of one more retelling and reliving of her treachery. But the tender-hearted and ever-patient Azena was always present, ready to pick her up when she woke. Who is this Azena? She's not related by blood to Marie, and she wasn't a friend of Marie's on earth. Aphraar tells us he was awed by her "angelic tenderness and unrestrained devotion." Azena lives on a higher plane and volunteered to come down to Marie's level from a feeling of compassion. Azena is a spirit putting her love into action. She could not have found the work easy or congenial. And she will leave Marie, we are told, when Marie is strong enough to carry on without her. At that point Azena will tell her story—joyously tell it, especially if the "mission" was successful—to her friends back on her own plane, and she will listen to them tell theirs. She will rest in the heavenly beauty and happiness of that plane for some time. Then she will gird her loins and take on the next case—all in the knowledge that her work as a "missionary of love" is the way to grow her soul and progress to more divine levels. There are many other ways to progress, and we'll look at them a little later, but this is Azena's.

It was also Frances Banks'. She descended into the Shadows, you will recall, to lead the French painter toward the light. She didn't win him over by displays of affection—that was not her style—but by a relentless, patient process of reasoning that in the end he could not prevail over. Along the way she suffered insult and abuse, but she never flinched. And when it was all over she led him out of the gloom with a feeling of deep satisfaction.

We see many similar cases in this literature. Here is one that is closer to home. Surely we all know someone like him; perhaps we recognize ourselves in him. Charles Henry Fryer, using his son's hand, writes:

I was given one very interesting person to visit; whom you would know by name if I were to give it.... Enough to say he was counted a sinner on your side, and was never regarded as a good man, yet there was goodness in him ... He was wandering in utter despondency when I found him, and at first it was hard to effect a contact. Then we were able to come to terms with each other by means of a common interest, and we talked of our love of nature, and his despair was of ever being able to enjoy the sight of trees or flowers again, for where I found him it was a desert of sand and had no charm or natural sweetness. For a long time we conversed, until at last he asked me why I was there, and I told him I was sent to restore his faith in God, and that he would be able to come to more refreshing regions if he could only trust me. So he said he would take me at my word, and I took him to a part of the second sphere where the boundaries are like the beauty of your own earth, and told him that beyond them there was sweetness and light, and that he was not excluded from them, but he must try to let his frozen heart reach out, and I would help him. The sight of his efforts was something I cannot forget. You can yourself appreciate his difficulty, and for me it was a test of my own spiritual powers. This is where we have to pray with all our might and help the unbelief of the one who has never learned to pray. And after a while his ability to pray began to come back to him, and I could tell that he would be able to come with me beyond the boundaries. He was emotionally very much moved, and said he did not ever think he could have got to his present state if I had not helped him, but I replied that I was only doing my duty, and he realized that was so, as he in his earthly life had understood what duty meant from his service in the army. So he came with me across the boundary, and I was able to put him into the company of his wife who had died before him, and I left them believing in God's love and profusely grateful.

This man was not a newcomer; he had been wandering lost for an unspecifiable time. Others, however, receive care as soon as they come over. This work can be tedious. Some caregiving is more rewarding than others! Here is a typical complaint—from Monsignor Benson:

> The percentage is low, deplorably low, of people who come into the spirit world with any knowledge at all of their new life and of the spirit world in general. All the countless souls without this knowledge have to be taken care of, and helped in their difficulties and perplexities. That is the principal work upon which Edwin, Ruth [his spirit friends] and I are engaged.

The worst cases involve those newly dead who need convincing they have really died. Benson continues: "I do assure you it is not a pleasant sight to see these gentle, patient [spirit] helpers wrestling mentally— and sometimes almost physically—with people who are wholly ignorant of the fact that they are 'dead'. "

At the opposite end of the spectrum are spirits of the innocent dead untouched by earth—toddlers, even stillborn babies. Zabdiel visits a "children's home" where such innocents were taken and raised by a husband and wife who stayed together after their deaths:

> These had the care of the children, boys and girls, who had been either stillborn, or who had died at birth or soon after. Such are not, as a rule, taken to those homes in the lower spheres, but brought higher [right away] for their development. This is because there is little of earth to do out of their natures; and they also need more special care than those who have, even by a little, fought and developed in the earth battle of life.

Leslie Stringfellow tells his mother,

> There are many homes for children here, and today we visited one situated in an immense grove of trees, and the buildings covered a space of ground as large as a small town.

This was for small children under seven and eight years. Older ones have other homes, where they go after leaving these infant ones.

The children are watched over and cared for by the most beautiful and motherly spirits who in their earth-life were especially fond of children. These are entirely orphans, as we call them, or children whose parents are still on earth, but who will take them home when they themselves come over.

Leslie doesn't do a bad job himself. On December 25, 1889, he organized a Christmas activity. He materialized a Christmas tree and supervised a party complete with music he composed and presents to give to the kids. He describes the scene:

Well, we had our tree. It was ornamented with real jewels as well as toys and we had little images of all kinds of birds and beasts. . . . The children all stood around and sang beautiful Christmas hymns, and when all the presents were off the tree, we dematerialized it, and it melted away into a green vapor, and disappeared.

It would be a mistake to think that heaven can't be fun! But more about this later.

One of the most surprising discoveries I've made about spirit life is their interest in us. But on second thought, why surprising? After all, we can't see their world, but they can see ours; and what we see we usually take seriously, while what we can't see we usually ignore. That simple fact explains why they are so much more interested in us than we are in them—that and the fact that they remember vividly what earth was like, having once lived there, often recently, whereas we, with our dense physical brains shutting out the light from above, usually remember nothing about where we came from. Let's look at a few examples of how the spirits serve us.

Most spirit accounts assure us that each of us has one or more spirit guardians or guides. Monsignor Benson devotes a fascinating chapter to them. "Every soul," he begins, "born upon the earth-plane has allocated to him—or her—a spirit guide." He continues, ". . . guides understand and are in sympathy with their charges' failings. Many of them indeed had the same failings when they were incarnate, and among other useful services they try to help their charges overcome those failings and weaknesses." Although "unknown to those they serve," spirit guides have a subtle influence over those entrusted to them, and "it is usually the spirit guide who has implanted the better thought within the brain." By what means? By "subtly instilled telepathic suggestions," Judge Hatch tells us. However, "It must never be thought for one instant that the influence of the spirit guide negatives the possession or expression of free will," Benson continues. Silver Birch is especially eloquent on this subject:

> Unseen, unheard, we do reach you, exercising a silent but yet real influence in your lives, guiding you, quickening you, striving to direct you, aiding you to make the right choice so that your characters will grow, your souls will evolve, and you will be led into those paths which will enable you to extract from life all that is necessary for your growth and understanding.

But more often than not the spirits fail. They tell us they do their best to instill telepathically some encouragement or warning or piece of advice, but all too often it is rejected, sometimes with grave results. Even worse, they sometimes have to work around dark spirits counseling in the opposite direction. Judge Hatch says: "The heavens above your head now are literally swarming with souls who long to take a hand in the business of earth, souls who cannot let go, who find the habit of managing other people's affairs a fascinating habit, as enthralling as that of tobacco or opium." Their presence in our world is vouched for in many other spirit accounts, and we'll devote a short chapter to them a little later. For now let's bear in mind that not all spirits who penetrate our world are loving helpers.

But back to those who are. These are not spirits bound to earth by selfish needs, but "souls who voluntarily linger around your earth," according to Imperator, "whose motive-spring is love." Helpful spirits always have our best interest at heart. They can inspire a melody for a composer or a discovery for a scientist. They can guide the hand of a surgeon or lead us to safety when we are lost. Spirits tell us they are the inspiration behind genius. Benson says, "Man can perform certain actions with precision and exactitude. He can paint a picture, he can play upon an instrument, he can manipulate machinery, but all the major discoveries that are of service to the earth-plane have come, and always will come, from the spirit word." Silver Birch adds, "You are all instruments, whether you are conscious of the fact or not. You receive and transmit. And according to the degree that you

make yourselves susceptible to spirit influence, so are you successful or not." Vale Owen's deceased mother tells us that "all your best
music comes to you . . . from trained workers who are constantly ac-
tive in giving earth some little gift of heavenly music." The great ro-
mantic composer Johannes Brahms, writing well before his death,
apparently agreed: "Straight-away the ideas flow in upon me, directly
from God, and not only do I see distinct themes in my mind's eye,
but they are clothed in the right forms, harmonies, and orchestra-
tion." If Brahms had been familiar with spirit communication, he
probably would have attributed his sublime melodies to spirit muses
rather than God. However, Astriel adds that spirits are careful not
to do too much. "If we did, then the benefit derived from your earth
schooling would be materially lessened."

Spirit help can also be very down-to-earth, even gritty. Soon after
his death A.D. Mattson caught up with his father, who had died many
years earlier, and told his incarnate daughter what he (her grandfather) had been doing:

> My father took me to see the results of the famine and the tidal
> wave in East Pakistan. [A typhoon sweeping up the Bay of Bengal
> in 1971 generated a wave that claimed 300,000 lives.] He seems to
> have adopted these people as his focal point of his serving. He has an
> uncanny awareness of their abilities and also of their basic tendency
> to procrastinate as long as they have enough for today. . . . He gets in
> touch with them [mostly through their dreams] and [telepathically]
> gives them little impressions to make them realize that the sun is high
> and it's time they got things done. . . . He has a fine group of associates
> with him who work to help them in their sleep.

Mattson's cousin, Bill Hoag, who died in 1942, "helps those [Viet-
nam] war casualties who still have to stay on earth and are not allowed
to come over just yet. This is a very tedious and very special kind of
work. These wounded people have to be given the courage and strength
to go on living, even though they may be badly crippled." Spirits like
Bill "are able to help the disabled when they are out of the body during sleep. They help them to have a positive attitude to go forward and
fight against the various problems that come with disability."

Another kind of service to earth's humans comes from spirits working through mediums—the teachers behind a book such as this. The
best of spirit communicators are driven by love for our sorrowing world.

Often they see the root of the problem in a materialist philosophy that denies the reality of spirit. Silver Birch is typical:

> At the root of all your evils is ... ignorance of spiritual law. Do you not realize that, once the gospel of materialism and all the self-interest it teaches is exploded forever, you have rid the world of its greatest curse? ... Men have built their lives upon false foundations. Nations have tried to organize their policies on the principle of national self-interest. Dictators have risen and have become tyrannical, only because they have been subservient to the gospel that might is right. Do you not see how necessary this knowledge is, not only to the individual, not only to the nation, but to the whole world?

The spirit who wishes to communicate with us, as we saw earlier, must descend into a region of slow vibration where the spirit's subtle mind must contend with earth's density. This is never easy, and sometimes spirits cry out in frustration. "Pardon me if I rarely use you," the spirit of Frederic Myers exclaims to one of his mediums. "I can't stand the way you bother." And Imperator chastises one of the most gifted mediums who ever lived, Stainton Moses. In their early communications, Moses, an Anglican priest, was troubled by Imperator's theology, which strayed from Christian orthodoxy. Imperator writes through Moses' hand, "... we cannot fail to know that at the root of [your objections] lies mistrust of our statements and want of confidence in our claims. This is painful to us, and, as we feel, unjust." And there is the additional frustration of being misrepresented. "Granted that discarnate communication is a possibility," writes Charles' Fryer's father; "nevertheless the communications have to be effected through a human being who is still enfleshed, and who cannot divest himself or herself of all his or her preconceptions and ingrained attitudes." Spirit communication is no easy job. At its best it's an act of self-sacrificing service to a confused world.

Many spirits tackle larger projects. Charles Fryer's father explains:

> We have also groups who are assigned to influencing the general operations of men and nations, and who help invisibly in the working of what you call nature. Those engaged in this work need to be combative, for there are evil influences to be withstood, and there are battles of will before a particular assignment is successfully carried out.

Some spirits turn their attention to even loftier concerns. Ambrose Pratt, a saint on earth according to those who knew him best, spoke of "an aspiration which can only be eventually attained through tremendous effort. I seek to become a member of the Divine Hierarchy of Souls who maintain and conserve the material universe." Here is a spirit who longs to serve, not men and nations, but the universe! Apparently there is no limit to what can be achieved by the humble sons and daughters of earth. There is no limit to our potential greatness.

Spirits sometimes wonder how earth manages to survive. Benson says that "had we withdrawn every element of our influence, the earth world would, in a very brief time, be reduced to a state of complete and absolute barbarity."

As mentioned earlier, though, many spirits show no interest in serving. Ambrose Pratt tells us these "unevolved souls . . . remain human personalities living in their desired picture of earth for many years (according to earth-time) on this side of the border. Usually they go no further on the upward way. They eventually reincarnate." They are not ready—yet—for the "Highlands of Heaven." They haven't developed the sense that they are "each other's keeper . . . all part of the ONE pulsating, living, glorious WHOLE," as AD Mattson puts it.

Aphraar marvels at "the tender sympathy and humility with which those higher, holier natures render assistance to the weaker. . . . Whatever they may have done," he continues, "they have a wonderful power and aptitude of making you feel—no matter how great your enjoyment has been—that by far the greater happiness has accrued to them."

13

Master Spirits, Messiahs, and Teachers

A lmost all of earth's religions revere exalted beings who function as masters, saviors, or gods. Most of them had an earthly origin, a personal history, but are now long departed, their lives recalled in sacred legend and myth. Jews have their prophets, Christians have their Jesus and their various saints, Hindus their avatars and seers, Muslims their Prophet and their pirs, Buddhists their Buddhas and bodhisattvas, and the Chinese their gods and ancestors. Turning to them for help and inspiration, even salvation, is basic to all our religions. They lift our hearts toward adoration as we contemplate their unique qualities. We commune with them. We aspire to be more like them. Though they live in a world far above ours, we hope that they notice us and bless us. Less than the Source, the Supreme, the All-Knowing, they nevertheless evoke our deepest wonder and love.

Is there anything like this in heaven?

There is.

"Shall I tell you of one whom I call the Beautiful Being?" wrote Judge Hatch through his medium Elsa Barker. "If it has a name in heaven, I have not heard it. Is the Beautiful Being man or woman? Sometimes it seems to be one, sometimes the other. There is a mystery here which I cannot fathom."

Hatch had been meditating and, for the first time since his death, had reached a state of rapture. Suddenly this strange being appeared:

Standing before me was the Beautiful Being, radiant in its own light. Had it been less lovely I might have gasped with wonder; but the very perfection of its form and presence diffused an atmosphere of calm. I marveled not, because the state of my consciousness *was* marvel. I was lifted so far above the commonplace that I had no standard by which to measure the experience of that moment.

Hatch would meet the Beautiful Being a second time, and they had a conversation:

"Is this the particular heaven where you dwell?" I asked.

"Oh, I dwell nowhere and everywhere," the Beautiful Being answered. "I am one of the voluntary wanderers, who find the charm of home in every heavenly or earthly place." . . .

"And do you love the earth?"

"The earth is one of my playgrounds. I sing to the children of earth sometimes; and when I sing to the poets, they believe that their muse is with them. Here is a song which I sang one night to a soul which dwells among men."

The Beautiful Being then sings a song for Hatch. Here is one of its stanzas, typical of the style of the poem as a whole: "I was young when the sun was formed, and I shall be young when the moon falls in the arms of her daughter the earth."

In one of the most extraordinary spirit chapters I've read, Hatch tells us more about this being:

I have written you before of one whom I call the Beautiful Being, one whose province seems to be the universe, whose chosen companions are all men and angelkind, whose playthings are days and ages.

For some reason, the Beautiful Being has lately been so gracious as to take an interest in my efforts to acquire knowledge, and has shown me many things which otherwise I should never have seen.

On one occasion the Beautiful Being guides him on a trip to earth. Moving from place to place, from scene to scene, it teaches Hatch as they move along. At one point the Beautiful Being touched his hand and whispered:

> "The life that is so sweet to these mortals is a book of enchantment for me."

> "Yet you have never tasted human life yourself?"

> "On the contrary, I taste it every day; but I only taste it—and pass on. Should I consume it, I might not be able to pass on."

> "But do you never long so to consume it?"

> "Oh, but the thrill is in the taste! Digestion is a more or less tiresome process." . . .

> "You irresistible one!" I cried. "Who are you? *What* are you?"

Hatch tell us, "Those who behold the Beautiful Being are never the same again as they were before." He cries out later, "I love you . . . with an incomprehensible love."

The Beautiful Being is lovable not for its goodness, but its beauty. He (I'll call him he from now on to emphasize his personhood) reminds me more of Krishna than Christ. He is certainly a force for good, but we don't see him struggling against evil. He changes people by inspiring in spirits like Hatch a delight they would not know otherwise. At one point Hatch affectionately calls him a "Divine wanton," a sort of heavenly version of Oscar Wilde. Witty, artistic, and bewitching, the Beautiful Being shows us that heaven is full of remarkable spirits waiting to help us in ways we can't even imagine.

How different from this playful master spirit is the other major force in Hatch's spirit life. Hatch calls him simply the "Teacher." Hatch is in awe of his power—"I have seen him command literally 'legions of angels.'" Hatch thinks of him as "one of the Christs . . . for the heart of my Teacher is very soft to the sufferings of the world." The Teacher then explains why he's not a Christ:

> Like the ministering angels, I go where I am most needed. Only the strong ones can learn what I have to teach. The weak ones are the charges of the Messiahs [like Jesus] and their followers. But,

nevertheless, between us and the Messiahs there is brotherhood and there is mutual understanding. Each works in his own field. The Messiahs help the many; we help the few. Their reward in love is greater than ours; but we do not work for reward any more than they do. Each follows the law of his being.

Not a Christ or a Messiah for the many, but a teacher for the few. That's what the Teacher makes plain to his student. Why was Hatch singled out? Following his death, a eulogy in the *Los Angeles Times* described Hatch as "a great man." He spent five years living as a hermit in "the wilds of British Columbia" before returning to the practice of law and to independent philosophical research. His longtime associate called him "a philosopher of the soul." It's perhaps not surprising, then, that "the Teacher" sought him out and trained him. My guess is that there are many teachers who come down from their perch to form the next generation of teachers. Hatch was far from unique in the attention he got.

We saw in a previous chapter that Ambrose Pratt dreamed of managing some aspect of the material universe in a future age when he was ready. We find references to such management in other accounts. Hatch, for example, tells us he's been told "that the guardian spirit of this planet Earth evolved himself into a god of tremendous power and responsibility in bygone cycles of existence." He then embarks on an extraordinary (for us) speculation:

Who do you fancy will be the gods of the future cycles of existence? Will they not be those who in this cycle of planetary life have raised themselves above the mortal? Will they not be the strongest and the most sublime among the present spirits of men? Even the gods must have their resting period, and those in office now would doubtless wish to be supplanted.

To those men who are ambitious for growth, the doors of development are always open.

Hatch is not only teaching us to think of highly evolved spirits in a new way; he is painting a breathtaking picture of our possible future. Allow me to speculate a little further and ask if Earth's "guardian spirit" has the power to steer the planet away from catastrophe in ways we can't imagine. If so, is it safe to assume he will interfere only as a last resort, and without our knowledge? How about global warming? Or an approaching asteroid? Many spirit accounts make it clear that spirits could do much more to solve our problems—at both the individual and the collective level—than they are allowed to.

A fairly common theme in spirit literature is "the visit." Ordinary spirits try to describe what it feels like to be in the presence of an august, godlike being who drops down from a high heaven to bless them. Monsignor Benson describes such a moment:

> ... we have our temples where we can receive the great messengers from the highest realms, fitting places to ... send our united thanks and our petitions ... to the Great Source of all.

> The building itself was magnificent. ... The sanctuary ... was filled with many beings from higher realms, with the exception of a space in the centre, which I guessed was reserved for our visitant. ... And in the centre there slowly took shape the form of our visitant. As it gained in density we could see that he was a man whose appearance was that of youth—spiritual youth—but we knew that he carried with him to an unimaginable degree the ... attributes of Wisdom, Knowledge, and Purity. ...

> It is not possible for me to convey to you one fraction of the exaltation of the spirit that I felt while in the presence, though distant, of this heavenly guest. But I do know that not for long could I have remained in that temple while he was there without undergoing the almost crushing consciousness that I was low, very, very low upon the scale of spiritual evolution and progression. And yet I knew that he was sending out to me, as to us all, thoughts of encouragement, of good hope, of kindness in the very highest degree ...

> With a final benediction upon us, this resplendent and truly regal being was gone from our sight.

Benson devotes the last chapter of his book to a journey he was allowed to take to one of the higher heavens. At first he is entranced by the beauty of the realm, its radiant mansions and palaces, its splendid gardens and trees, its river flowing alongside the magnificent buildings "far away into the distance." He contrasts the "heavy-looking materials of our own realm" to the "crystalline substance" from which the buildings now before him were made.

Far from being aloof and superior, as Benson and his companions feared, the residents of this place were welcoming: "As we walked down the corridors we met and were greeted by the most friendly and gracious beings. . . . There was no coldness, but everywhere the warmth of friendliness and affection." When brought into the presence of the ruler, again there was no standing on ceremony:

> But, strange as it may sound, though we had been transported unfathomable distances to the presence of this transcendingly wonderful being, yet here in his very presence we felt perfectly at home, perfectly at ease with him. He laughed with us, he joked with us, he asked us what we thought of his roses . . . . He spoke to each of us individually, displaying an exact acquaintance with all our concerns, collectively and personally.

The rules of earth which protect the dignitary from the mob do not apply to the heavenly realms. The reason is that egotism is a ticket downward, not upward. The higher the spirit, the less the need for pomp and ceremony. Humility reigns, and service is close behind. Zabdiel tell us that "each Angel-guide [is] accountable for, and identified with, the one, or the community, over which he is placed to serve. He enjoys with them, and suffers with them; he rejoices over them, and mourns over their shortcomings." The usual bowing and scraping before celebrity is so out of place in the courts of heaven that Azena didn't think twice about referring to the illustrious Cushna, you might remember, as "dear old Doctor Grand-pa."

Another type of spiritual master is the leader of the so-called Group Soul. Many spirits are members of large spirit families, or "Group Souls," that are waiting for them when they pass. They feel as if they have come home when they are received by the familiar group. Frances Banks tells us that souls in a Group are "part of ourselves. Their connection with us is deeper and far more permanent than mere earth contacts could make it." Ambrose Pratt explains that "the members of each group are inter-related and make a pattern. Discarnate and incarnate souls belong to a group. Though individualized on the earth-plane and seemingly isolated units, on the deeper level they share a common unconscious." Group Souls are usually specialty groups, not family groups. The spirit Frederic Myers uses an example from music:

If a certain type of psyche is continually being evolved in the one group, you will find that eventually that type, if it be musical, will have a musical genius as its representative on earth. It will harvest all the tendencies in those vanished lives, and it will then have the amazing unconscious knowledge that is the property of genius.

In a Group Soul a powerful "informing spirit makes these souls one," Myers says. Frances Banks explains:

> Since I have left the earth life I have been taught by a Teacher with whom I am in contact, mentally and spiritually. He Himself is a part of the Group Soul in the Group towards which I am progressing. . . . This teacher is a higher Disciple, a wise and advanced soul, and is able to impart knowledge and wisdom to souls in the Group.

Mostly he is absent from the Group, since he lives in a much higher realm than the other members. She explains further: "He fulfills the role of Director of their work and study. He visits them, it seems, when there is a new impulse in their researches to be studied and tested," or when a new candidate is to be "interviewed and judged ready for admission." Unfortunately, Banks doesn't tell us what the Group focus is.

The chapter wouldn't be complete without a reference to the most exalted spiritual type mentioned in spirit literature (excluding the Supreme Source or Godhead). We turn again to Myers:

> You dwell not only outside of time but outside of the universe on this last plane of being. Yet you can be and are, in one sense, within the universe. You as part of the Whole—and by the Whole I indicate God—may be likened to the sun; your rays pervade the material universe, yet your spirit remains detached from it, reigning in the great calm of eternity.

> [In this condition] you are wholly aware of the imagination of God. So you are aware of every second in time, you are aware of the whole history of the earth from Alpha to Omega. Equally all planetary existence is yours. Everything created is contained within that imagination, and you . . . know it and hold it.

Myers tells us these superspirits are inaccessible; no ordinary spirit would think to ask them for help; as Myers puts it, they are "Out

Yonder." Yet they do serve in their own way. Just by being who they are, their example and influence are felt throughout creation: their "rays pervade the material universe."

What is remarkable about this final category of being is that we can reach this height. On the other hand, most of us, Myers explains, wouldn't want to! To do so would mean becoming "perfect," and few spirits reach this high. Most feel that this degree of perfection comes at too high a price.

Judge Hatch wants us never to forget that the will is free. No one is forced to scale a height beyond his or her aspiration. On the other hand, the invitation to progress, while never imposed, is never withdrawn. Hatch sums up the process:

> Humanity on its long road has evolved many Masters. Who then shall dare to question that humanity has justified itself? If one demands to know what purpose there is in life, tell him that it is this very evolution of the Master out of the man. Eternity is long. The goal is ahead for each unit of sufficient strength, and those who cannot lead can serve.

14

Prayer

rayer is a reverential act of communication with a presence that our five senses can't pick up – a spiritual presence. This presence is conceptualized on earth in many different ways. These range from one's deceased ancestors to the spirits of great men to gods and goddesses of various rank to a Supreme Person who loves, protects, and heals his or her creation to a Cosmic Consciousness that pervades and unites the universe. These unseen realities are often pictured – painted, sculpted, sketched, described. Most people who pray picture in their imagination the target of their prayer. Even those who don't consciously rely on a picture usually imagine something – perhaps a luminous oblong blur or the sound of the name they give it. The question before us is this: Do spirits in the afterworld engage in this kind of activity? Do they send forth prayer to those above them, and do they receive and answer and sometimes even benefit from prayer coming up from below?

William James during his life on earth believed devoutly in the value and blessedness of faith but never completely succeeded in overcoming his doubts regarding the truth of religion, the reality and nature of God, and the reality of an afterlife; he was not attached to any church or religion, and there is no indication in his writings that he prayed. By contrast, Drayton Thomas's sister, Etta, was a Christian with a strong belief in the world to come and, we have every right to assume, a well developed prayer life. Placed side by side, they look very different. But in the afterworld where they now dwell—he died in 1910, she in 1920— they begin to look much more alike.

Each has a relation to the Ultimate. Each has what we might call a prayer life. But they go about it in different ways. "Father and I go together to a meeting for prayer," Etta says. She goes on to tell of "thanksgiving services which we have here." Outwardly Etta is doing the same kind of thing she did on earth as a Christian. But there is a big difference: "one's condition here makes prayer so much more wonderful than anything one knows on earth, much more so." James, you might recall, spoke of God as an Atmospheric Presence that knows him more intimately than he knows himself. James is sure "that it possesses a psychology far divorced from any with which I have ever been acquainted"; it "lends itself actively to seek my good in the most particular and individual ways"; and "it spontaneously delivers what is needed before I realize my own needs—in a way more characteristic of a mother, say, than a father." This is not the language of conventional theism. Can his relation to the Atmospheric Presence be described, then, as prayerful? Comparing himself to a weary traveler, he writes:

On occasion, caught in a mood of disappointment or weariness, he [the traveler] shouts out mentally for help. Remarkably enough, he is provided with an otherwise inexplicable boon: sudden energy or health or the solution to a problem.... But what strikes him most is his feeling that someone or something in the universe is cheering him on, that some kind of power exists outside of his present course of events, and when he calls upon it, that power can insert itself [and] transform his reality to some extent....

James never uses the word "prayer," but it's clear that what he's doing fits our definition. Jane Roberts, his medium, concluded that James's Atmospheric Presence "is responsive and actively *wants* to give support" and that it helps if we "state our needs or intents."

Etta Thomas, the trusting Christian, has no trouble taking her needs to her God. In almost childlike simplicity she tells her brother:

Since being over here I have learnt, more than I ever understood while on earth, that God likes to be talked to. I will express it just so. Supposing that while living at home you had gone in and out, keeping apart from your father and me and never consulting us. We should not have liked that; the more you consulted us the more pleased we were. God is like that. We should remember that we are His children. He could do everything without us, but He likes being asked to help.

Whether the Master of the Universe really does take note of Etta's prayers in the way she imagines can be questioned—she is not infallible. But what can't be questioned is the prevalence of prayer lifted toward the highest heights in adoration, trust, love, and thanksgiving. In this respect she is not so different from James.

Many Protestant Christians believe that praying to anyone but God is a mistake. But they are very likely to change their minds once they've died, for there is a great deal of praying *between* spirits. Typically, a spirit in a higher sphere may pick up a cry for help from a suffering relative or friend in a lower sphere—perhaps the Shadowlands—and come to that unfortunate spirit's aid. Or a spirit may hear a call from earth. Prayers addressed to "God" or "Father" or "Allah" or "Krishna" or "Jesus" serve as flares that alert the spirit with a tie to the one praying that help is needed—spirits are often eager to help their loved ones back on earth. Or a prayer from earth might be picked up by a spirit who is being prayed for, and that can bring happiness to the spirit. For example, a prayer from earth asking mercy from God for Uncle Fred lets Uncle Fred know that he is being remembered and loved by his niece—aside from whatever divine aid the prayer might ignite. These exchanges of love and caring are ubiquitous in spirit literature.

Here are a few examples. The first two show how anguished prayer is picked up by rescuing spirits from those dwelling in "realms of darkness." Charles Fryer's father explains:

> . . . we have freedom to enter all spheres below our own, and to speak and converse with their inhabitants whenever the time is suitable. They are not able to come to us unless we first go to them, but they do have the ability to ask for us in a sort of prayer which they can put out. We may not be able to come at once, and our inability to do so may be due to the fact that we are deliberating, or to the fact that the most useful person in a group is occupied with helping someone else. So we may have to delay for a short time before going where we are prayed for. We see from many signs around us that one or another of us is needed, and the usual thing is for a quick meeting to be held, and a decision made as to who shall go.

Here is a second explanation, this from Zabdiel:

> When a spirit leaves a dark region for one less dark he experiences an immediate sense of relief and comfort by comparison with his former

state. For now his environment is in harmony with his own inner state of development. But as he continues to develop in aspiration after good, he gradually becomes out of harmony with his surroundings, and then, in ratio to his progress, so his discomfort increases until it becomes … agony. Then in his helplessness, and approaching near to despair, having come to that pass when his own endeavors can go no further, he cries out for help to those who are able to give it in God's Name, and they enable him one stage onward nearer to the region where dimness, rather than darkness, reigns. And so he at last comes to the place where light is seen to be light, and his onward way is henceforth not though pain and anguish, but from joy to greater joy, and hence to glory and glory greater still.

Spirit literature presents us with many accounts of compassionate service to fellow spirits who call out a prayer for help.

Even more attention is given to prayers that come up from earth. They come in two forms: prayers for help with some earth-based problem, and prayers for the wellbeing of a deceased relative or friend.

Etta Thomas explains how prayer from earth is picked up:

His thoughts provide a kind of lead which we can follow and so accomplish what we might not otherwise be able to do. You know what a paper-chase is. Well, this is like laying a trail with his thoughts and we follow the little scraps of paper and get hot on the scent, and if we follow closely we can usually help with those about whom we are thinking.

Etta is saying that if Carol is praying for David, she can usually make contact with David and give him help if he permits it.

The advanced spirit Imperator goes into more detail:

True prayer is the ready voice of spirit communing with spirit; the cry of the soul [on earth] to invisible friends with whom it used to speak. … It is the placing of a suffering soul in union with a ministering spirit who can soothe and heal. It needs no words, no attitude, no form. It is truest when these are absent, or at least unstudied. It needs only a recognition of a near guardian, and an impulse to communion. To this end it must be habitual; else, like the limb long disused, the impulse is paralysed. … Pray, then; but see that you pray not with formality, heartlessly, and with unreal supplication. Commune with us.

Vale Owen's mother explains to her son that many—probably almost all—of earth's prayers addressed to God are picked up by spirits. God is out of the loop, not because He lacks love, but because, as we saw above, he assists souls through other souls. In that way not only is the receiver benefited but the giver is empowered—a win-win situation, as we say.

Most of us are aware, if we are honest with ourselves, that our prayers often—perhaps usually—don't deliver what we ask for. Why is this? Dr. Andre Luiz, a spirit communicating through the renowned Brazilian medium Chico Xavier, explains that those prayed for

> receive what they need. Many ask for their bodies to be healed, but we are forced to consider to what extent this might be useful for them . . . others request guidance of various types, obliging us to balance our work so as not to hinder individual freedom. Earthly existence is an active spiritual preparation course and almost always there is no lack of lazy students in the school, who waste time instead of making the most of it, and who are anxious for false achievements that require the least amount of effort. For this reason, in the area of guidance, the majority of the requests go unheeded.

Luiz is saying that many of us waste time on frivolous activities and that the only antidote to this lazy habit is a crisis of some kind—a crisis is often the only way to make us take life seriously and give it our best. If we are one of those lazy souls, then when we pray for a solution to the crisis, we are in actuality praying for a return to the old habit of an easy, drifting, unchallenging lifestyle. Helper spirits will therefore not cooperate. They love us too much to intervene and remove the very challenge that is calling forth our best effort and building our character. In Chapter 6 I used the analogy of earth as a "moral gymnasium." That analogy applies here.

There are plenty of times, on the other hand, when help from above is deserved. And spirits are eager to give it when asked. But giving help is an art that must be studied and mastered. Thus there are schools in the heavens for dedicated healers. Luis describes such a "Center":

> The Center prepares spirits for the purpose of transforming them into "living letters" of rescue and aid to other spirits who are suffering . . . on earth's surface. Our [training] is a copy of the type of service that is being carried out in the most diverse spirit cities of the higher planes.

Many, many spirits are prepared here to spread hope and consolation, and to provide instruction and counsel in the various arenas of the planet's evolution.

AD Mattson devotes a chapter to the subject of prayer. "When you, on earth," he says, "are feeling depressed, those in the unseen realms who are joyous and are sending light can make a link with you and can help to lift you." He then describes what impact a prayer group has on the spirit world:

> When you start to pray, we receive and pass on and act as boosters or assistants in your praying. Our power and your power together become more tangible to you than just yours alone. Each prayer group has its own guardians and helpers from the unseen realm. These guardians and helpers, in turn, receive power from you.

All this sending and receiving works by telepathy. In fact, all prayer is telepathic—invisible, inaudible mind-to-mind communication without dependence on the power of vocalized speech. Telepathy is a slippery subject, however, and many humans don't believe in it. But all spirits in the heavenly realms definitely do and use it all the time. Spirits know that once we die, there will be no more doubts!

Not all "downpourings of prayer" from spirits have an impact, however. Many times individuals or communities are "so shut in on themselves that the power just bounces back," Mattson says.

Finally, spirits are often on the receiving end of prayers sent their way from earth. Catholics down through the centuries have had masses said for their beloved dead thought to be suffering in Purgatory. A central feature of the religion of most Chinese throughout history has been praying for their ancestors. Hindu ritual offerings memorializing the dead sometimes stretch out for years following death. Even Protestant Christians, in spite of their belief that the dead don't need prayers said on their behalf, since they are either in unending hell where prayer would be pointless or in heaven where no amount of praying could improve their state, sometimes pray for the dead anyway. Anglicans, for example, say every Sunday, "We pray for all who have died, that they may have a place in your eternal kingdom."

But does all this praying do any good? Do spirits derive any benefit from earth's loving concern for them?

Spirits tell us our loving thoughts for them—often reaching them in the form of a prayer—are deeply appreciated. If the prayer is addressed to God or a lesser deity or a canonized saint on the deceased's behalf, this poses no problem. The prayed-for spirit picks up the intention behind the prayer directly, knows who is doing the praying, and is comforted. If forgotten by their earth friends and family, spirits can experience loneliness. Stringfellow tells his parents how much he appreciates their decorating his grave with flowers, then adds, "These little attentions delight your spirit friends, but alas, how many thousands of the loved but absent ones never receive the gift of a single flower." One of the spirits that Allan Kardec, the founder of Spiritism, worked with explains:

> [Your] Prayer . . . is a great source of comfort for the spirit you are praying for. To this spirit, your prayers show that you care, that it is not suffering [remorse] alone. Moreover, your interest could also encourage the afflicted spirit [in the Shadowlands] to seriously reconsider its attitude; such introspection might, by itself, shorten its sorrows.

Frances Banks makes the same point in her own way:

> Prayer and good thoughts for those who have left the earth, by their fellows still in incarnation, are a great aid to our work here. The prayer forms, and the potency of good thoughts, cause a quickened vibration to reach the one prayed for. As he is generally closely connected with his former life by interests and affections and memories, he is able to respond to such vibrations; thus he is much helped. Such petitions and meditations could be likened to a draught of healing water for the newly transmitted soul.

She then adds, concerning the ex-Nazi mentioned earlier, "But alas, there is no one on earth to pray for the repose of this poor soul." This lack of support makes her work more difficult. Ideally heaven and earth work in tandem.

Methodist Christians don't offer prayers for the deceased in their Sunday worship service or even their funeral service. One of my friends is a Methodist minister, and when I shared my research with him, he was torn between the doctrine of his church and the (alleged) advice of spirits. A compassionate man, the spirits won out—"just in case." My friend perhaps achieved a lesser result, unknown to him, by holding his beloved dead in loving memory. But in that case the intent to communicate was not present, and intention seems to be a catalyst in uniting the two worlds.

Prayer is a prominent feature in the life of spirits. They are encouraged to send it to those in need and to receive it when they are in need.

15

Worship and Celebration

On earth many of us gather in groups, even large groups, to worship God or celebrate a sacred event. These gathering places have names like synagogue, church, mosque, temple, gurdwara, shrine, meeting house, sweat lodge, and the like. Sometimes we gather in stadiums or out in nature, as at Stonehenge on the summer solstice. What we mean by God and might be celebrating might differ, but the need to cluster with others of like mind is universal. The question arises: Do spirits gather in groups to celebrate their faith?

AD Mattson, the Lutheran minister and theologian, devoted a chapter to worship. Speaking in the early 1970s through Margaret Flavell, the gifted British medium who helped trace downed fighter pilots during world War II, Mattson said, "We also have tremendous prayer meetings here, through which we mutually uplift each other. I had not realized how important worship of this kind would continue to be." Furthermore, "On the astral plane we still have great cathedrals and great churches. Ministers who preached on earth, and still feel the urge to do so, continue to preach here. I am one of those." Ian Currie, communicating through Muriel Williams between 1992 and 2002, elaborated:

> If you were a religious leader on the earth and you wish to continue on this course, your free will allows you to do so. If you want to talk on your faith, or listen to those of another denomination, it is your

prerogative; you will continue until you no longer require that religious calling. Those who lived earthly life through their faith will probably surround themselves in the afterlife with the same symbols and treasures that satisfied their beliefs.

Although most spirit communications come to us from Christian sources, we get glimpses of other faiths. On one of his astral travels Leslie Stringfellow entered a mosque: "There was an immense crowd assembled, and overhead a great cloud of vapor arose, and there was a platform on which were seated a lot of men in fine robes." An interesting side note was his discovery that Muslim women shared the mosque with the men and even had their heads uncovered. On further travel to an Indian sector he came across "large temples where were collected thousands of spirits who had been priests of Buddha and Brahma on earth." He noted that Hindu priests "spend a larger part of their time silently meditating in these temples."

Some spirit accounts make no mention of collective worship. William James, for example, seems content to spend most of his time alone. At the other end of the spectrum we find spirits who rhapsodize over being a small part of a vast ritual. Aphraar devotes twenty pages to such a ritual, a ceremony of healing. All I can hope to do here is suggest in some small way the grandeur, immensity, and emotional intensity of the event. In this description we see heaven opening up.

The venue is a vast open plane where recently deceased souls, not yet awakened from death, have been laid out on "couches." These souls have been victimized by oppressors of various kinds. "Wasted opportunities, wasted intellects, wasted lives!" Aphraar's guide tells him. Around them an immense arena stretches outward and upward. The healing ritual is about to begin. A massive sound of music, a chorale, fills the space. Aphraar describes the gathering crowd:

> Rapidly that spacious auditorium was filling up its seats. Tier after tier, rising one above another, contributed to that sea of faces, all lit up by happiness. From each of the four entrances a steady stream poured in until the hall was full.... The dresses worn were of many colours, but only of the lighter shades; all serving to make the groupings as picturesque as they were varied. The lower seats were filled by children wearing robes of spotless white, or tints of the most unimaginable delicacy; some of the wearers of such tender age as to make me wonder how they kept in the quiet order that everywhere prevailed....

Every nation upon earth had its legitimate representation in that throng, and all were so disposed that each complexion added its own influence to the balance of the picture. But the most pleasing thought of all was that every voice would say "Our Father" to the self-same God, and feel at heart that they were members of one family. The Jew was not conscious of his election, the Gentile had lost his hatred [of the Jew], the caste restriction of the Brahmin was broken down, the hand of the Arab was no more against his fellow. The Hindoo woman had doffed her veil, the Mohammedan had lost his bigotry, Greek and Roman thought not of deadly feuds, the hand of the Zulu held no assegai, the Indian hand no tomahawk, while the Christian had sheathed his sword. Romanist and Protestant gave the preference to each other, the Episcopalian boasted of no apostolic succession, and the narrow-minded sectarian sat side by side with the former atheist, whom he had before consigned to fire eternal. In such a multitude, with such a bond uniting them, I could fancy that I was not very far removed from the inner shrine of heaven.

The victims, still sleeping, have astral bodies twisted grotesquely into almost inhuman shapes that reflect the damage done to their in-dwelling spirits. The mystic energies produced by the crowd under the guidance of the leading healer I won't attempt to describe, but the excitement building up as the moment of awakening approaches I will.

A highly advanced spirit descends into the midst of the crowd. Aphraar describes him:

> I loved him the instant I beheld him.... In him were blended strength and gentleness like a bed of down on a granite rock, which emphasized every quality a man would desire to find in a cherished friend. From his eyes love and patience streamed in a steady, ebbless flow, his mouth breathed the fragrance of fidelity and affection.... He was a monarch, but his kingship was of service, and his prowess had been gained in lifting up the fallen.

Then follows the crowning event, the climax the audience, and especially Aphraar, have been waiting for:

> Over one and then another he bent his radiant form, loosing the influence of the refreshing spell which still caressed them, and as their eyes opened upon the bewildering scene around, he caught

each revived soul in his strong embrace, lifted it to his feet, and bade it welcome into a life of sympathy and compensation [for the wrongs done it on earth]. The revelation and recognition of the truth were simultaneous. It was simply a glance of enquiring wonder, followed by a smile of inexpressible joy, and all was over.

While earth's natives sit in bleachers at a NASCAR event hoping for a fatal crash—such is earth's lust for blood—the audience of spirits longs for something else. For them there is nothing so exciting as that moment when crippled, despairing souls, just arrived from earth, awake for the first time to an understanding of where they are. Only beings governed by love can thrill to such a moment.

The most striking description of collective spirit worship that I've come across reaches us in 1966 from Frances Banks, the former Anglican nun. The purpose of the "Ceremony of Light" is to mingle with and be transformed by an awesome, knowing, loving light. The transformation is accomplished through music on a grander scale than ever earth has known. All present are united in a prodigious effort to reach a particular Note (intentionally capitalized). Once reached, it "is held and *vibrated* at a pitch of intensity which sweeps every soul into harmony. The Light breaks through into the assembly. Light surrounds us, lifts us, touches, awakens us." She wants us to understand that the assembly is singing not only with their voices but with their whole organisms—whatever that means—so extraordinary is the experience.

Her descriptive powers cannot begin to suggest the degree of exaltation that she, and everyone else, feels. All she can say is that holding in consciousness that Note is the means of becoming united with "the vast World of Spirit." She ends her description with short, jagged sentences, each a paragraph in itself, barely comprehensible, as if stammering. Yet they manage well to convey the difference between our world and hers—the essential indescribability of her world in the languages of earth.

Another kind of ceremony marks the graduation of spirits to a higher sphere. A great multitude gathers to witness the elevation. Music and heraldry surround the event. Aphraar describes such an occasion. The leader, an "angel chief" of indescribable majesty with his attendants gathered round him, preaches a sermon without a word being spoken, at least not outwardly. Those who understand the sermon will be elevated. The great majority, including Aphraar, "stood and listened to the unbroken and profound peace that dwelt therein, but heard not the voice of the Father speaking; this was the test, the standard by which to measure the souls to be promoted." In other words, those who heard the voice in the silence were the ones worthy of promotion. When the silence ended, a great Amen sounded and all felt that "some great mysterious change had taken place; that some had passed again, not from death, but from life into life more abundantly." The ceremony closed when "another company of immortals descended from the hills on my right to the plain, chanting a song of welcome, to the friends they were to accompany to their new home.... the chosen ones arose, were joined by the choir above, and the festival was over." It's worth noting that Aphraar shows his humanness when he wonders, "given the fact that eternal progression of the soul was the law, and every angel in heaven had once been a man, how long would it require for one in my position to reach the point at which [the leader] stood."

In another ceremony tens of thousands watch as Jesus, referred to as "the Son of Man," conducts an elevation ceremony. Our old friend Zabdiel, a Christian in earth life, is one of those chosen. He and the others will be graduating from the Tenth to the Eleventh Sphere. The Son of Man, wearing on his head a crown of eleven stars, addresses the worthy: "Not perfectly have you served the Father and Me; but as you were able so you did your work. I ask no more than you do after this manner in the wider sphere of service into which I now call you." Once again we see that with elevation comes more responsibility, not rest, not "break time."

Other Christian celebrations are decidedly less solemn. Canadian Ian Currie, a professor of sociology at the University of Toronto, had a long-standing interest in psychical research. So it's not surprising that he would communicate to his friends from the Other Side. His account reminds us that there is a lot of fun to be had in heaven, especially on feast days:

Hello there [he is speaking to Bill Williams, a friend and fellow psychical researcher living in Toronto], I can't hear myself think for all the Irish folk here in spirit celebrating their St. Patrick Day!! They will have a great party "tonight" or perhaps I should say "all night" which is probably more accurate. I think I'll join in, I like a party. Now I bet you're thinking—what a load of rubbish! Just wait till you people pass on to this spirit plane; when you do, you will remember my words. Of course it is never "night" here; the light that surrounds us is wonderful, but not from the sun.

Currie also reminds us how often the eyes of spirits are trained back on earth: "I attended a wonderful ceremony of prayer and love here for the Pope when he became ill. I witnessed the light beaming to the earth, because of the love being projected from spirit. Also, there was a similar but simpler gathering for Mother Theresa when she became ill."

There is no doubt that spirits frequently gather in groups to worship and celebrate. They are a social lot. They even participate in *our* celebrations! AD Mattson explains:

> People in the astral realm are often attracted back to their churches on earth, and they find tremendous pleasure in giving color and light and love to the congregation that they have left. They, in turn, receive strength and help from those in that congregation when they are thought of and are remembered and are prayed for. Therefore, prayers for the departed members of a congregation should be a vital part of every worship service.

A final note. It would be a great mistake to associate the heavenly realms with endless worship, as many a Christian has done from too literal a reading of the Book of Revelation in the New Testament. Monsignor Benson makes this very point:

> We do not inhabit a land that bears all the outward marks of an Eternal Sunday! Indeed, Sunday has no place, no existence even, in the great scheme of the spirit world. We have no need to be forcibly reminded of the Great Father of the Universe, by setting aside one day to Him, and forgetting Him for the rest of the week. We have no week. With us it is eternal day, and our minds are fully and perpetually conscious of Him, so that we can see His hand and His mind in everything that surrounds us.

You might recall that William James, using untraditional, non-theistic language, makes a similar point about the "atmospheric presence." He says, "This presence is responsive. I am sure that it reacts to me, yet while it is everywhere, it is not obtrusive but again, like the summer day, it is more like a delightful medium in which all living is bathed so that it is quite possible to forget it almost, or take it for granted." In his sizable account James never refers to collective worship, probably because he was not a Christian in the habit of churchgoing. Yet his love of the "presence" is the most pervasive and interesting part of his narrative. I am left wondering if a spirit like James would have found the Ceremony of Light described by Frances Banks attractive. Or is he to be a loner to the end? We'll have to ask him when our time comes if he's still around!

16

Exaltation, Ecstasy, Endless Evolution

Earth's religions look forward to a blissful conclusion in the afterlife, either right away or eventually. If a religion fails to instill in the faithful the expectation of such a future, it rapidly declines. Contemporary Judaism is a case in point; most Jews, perhaps a majority, play down the importance of life after death and see it as otherworldly and escapist. And Judaism is not growing; a few years ago Sikhism passed it in numbers, and Mormonism, with its vivid afterlife teachings, will overtake it in a few more years. Christians who call themselves "progressive" tend in the same direction as their Jewish brothers, and their numbers are falling fast. Islam is the world's fastest growing major religion, and its full-blown confidence in a blissful afterlife—and fear of "the fire" if Paradise is lost— is the driving force behind its growth. Evangelical Christians have similar hopes and fears. (This is not meant to endorse Earth's more sinister afterlife beliefs or to demean the great accomplishments of Jews in our world.)

Do spirits in the astral realms look forward to a transcendental climax, an ecstasy or state of exaltation, presently out of their reach? Is their spiritual progress in the lower heavens driven by such a longing? And if so, how do they visualize the end point? Do they all see it the same way? And do they get hints of it from time to time—hints that inspire expectations of an Infinity beyond all endings? Is this yearning for infinity an important part of their lives?

Many souls see with great clarity how much growth lies ahead of them. Etta Thomas is a case in point. We've just seen how wonderful her experiences are, but she nevertheless sees herself as a work in progress. She is grateful for the changes wrought in her and expects more:

> . . . the four years since I passed over have gone very quickly and very happily. I grow more conscious of the wonderful things around me, things of which I was not wholly conscious at first. For instance, my range of sight and hearing, as well as understanding, is constantly increasing.

Other spirits look ahead to a future that almost takes one's breath away.

Frances Banks sees herself as embedded in a family of souls—what she calls a Group Soul (see Chapter 13)—that is evolving toward "the eternal Centre of Light and Creative Energy which men call God. . . . In this progressive creation," she continues, "we progress onwards and upwards into that Divine Self, after aeons of endeavor, into inclusion in the Divine Company, into bliss which is inexplicable at our present stage of understanding." She is aware that she is already on the upward path, for she finds herself sloughing off her astral body in favor of a "Body of Light." This body is "brilliant, 'encelled' with Light, ethereal in that there is no weight, no dragging down into matter but is enmeshed with colour and beauty . . ." Later she adds, "I feel as though I am starting on a Path of Light which leads . . . into Realms of unimaginable beauty and wonder and of which I have, as yet, but the faintest glimmer of comprehension."

But it's not just a young spirit like herself, dead only five months, who travels this path:

> . . . great Beings of Light [there are] who do the Will of the Divine Creator and who carry and transmit Power and Beauty and Light. But they too are in the process of progress, advancement toward their own great [Group] Centres. All is order, advancement, progress. And all is unity. Life cells within Life Cells, centres within Centres, groups within Groups, into the very Heart of Divinity.

Aphraar meets a woman he knew on earth who dedicated herself to the care of children in London's slums, and who wrote poetry on the side. "Thank God, I can and do still write," she exclaims. She recites a poem a page long full of spiritual fervor. In it she tells us why she must be satisfied with her present station in a lower heaven:

> Oh! the vision would o'erpower us,
> If it suddenly were given
> So we wait in preparation,
> In the vestibule of Heaven.

Aphraar, who died just a few weeks earlier and is still a novice, then asks her if "there are still other preparatory stages before you reach the final home":

> Oh, yes! There are others, how many I have no idea. The question which sometimes occurs to me is: Shall we ever reach the last? Is there a final? Since God is infinite, is it possible for us to arrive at any limit? Think how far we were from holiness when we commenced our pilgrimage on earth, and what a trifling distance we have yet travelled, then you will understand that there must yet be innumerable such stages before we can hope to stand in the undimmed splendour of His presence. With the new powers and greater knowledge which my new life has given me, unfolding a wider conception of His purity and my own unworthiness, I sometimes think it will be almost necessary for the remembrance of our earth life to pass away before we can bear to look upon His face.

Drayton Thomas's father shares this woman's vision. God's purpose, he says, is to give each soul endless opportunities to perfect itself:

> . . . one cannot attain a stage at which one can say, "There is nothing more to will, I must go on exactly as I am." Because when we master what we think is the absolute crowning point of knowledge in any subject, we immediately find that it has opened out a world of new knowledge again. You see it all around you. The possibilities over here are infinitely greater! On earth there are always many standing still: I do not expect them to see what I mean. But others will understand, those to whom light upon one point means a rising up to glimpse another field of exploration. There is no point of perfection which we can reach where there is nothing more to learn; there will always be this glorious sense of adventure in understanding and trying to

understand, following up and achieving. I do not lose my zest for more knowledge and enlightenment, it increases.

In this and previous quotations we see an endlessly expansive future for any soul desiring to know more, love more, and be more. We get glimpses of indescribable joy; and the degree of joy is proportionate to the development of noble character—a soul delighting in truth, goodness, and beauty. We should bear in mind, however, that many spirits are no more interested in spiritual advancement than they were on Earth. "There are sluggards and dull people here, as with you," Judge Hatch reminds us. "Most souls are nearly as blind as they were on earth." But there are plenty of teachers "who stand ready to help anyone who wishes their help in making real and deep studies in the mysteries of life."

Those earthlings blessed with a near-death experience (NDE) sometimes meet what they call a formless Being of Light full of love and understanding. Some even call the being God. I seriously doubt they are meeting God. It's much more likely that a "Being of Light" is an advanced soul putting into good use his or her talents—talents developed over many years, even centuries, of practice in the heaven worlds. One day we ourselves may be a being of light. For many of us that would require a complete overhaul of character.

Our potential is almost infinite. It's an exciting prospect.

17

The Dark Side

We all know that earth is full of people who pollute and threaten our environment. The many faces of evil leer at us daily from our TVs, newspapers, and ipads. They fascinate and horrify us. And they make our world a dangerous place to live in.

We saw earlier that the afterworld is a world of strict justice. We are accountable there for all that we do here, both good and bad. We've gotten more than a glimpse of what happens to evil people once they die. They suffer. But do they retain the ability to make others suffer? Can they inflict harm on other spirits, and can they inflict it on us? We've already seen that they can, but the topic of spirit malevolence needs a fuller development. I should warn you that you might not like what you read in this chapter.

Monsignor Benson describes a visit that he and two companions took to "the lower realms of the spirit world." They worked their way downward into a "gigantic crater many miles in circumference" half hidden in darkness and took a position slightly above the floor of the crater. This is what they saw:

> The inhabitants were variously occupied: some were seated on small boulders, and gave every appearance of conspiring together, but upon what devilish schemes it was impossible to say. Others were in small groups perpetrating unspeakable tortures upon the weaker of their kind who must, in some fashion, have fallen afoul of their tormentors. Their shrieks were unbearable to listen to, and so we closed our ears to them,

firmly and effectively. Their limbs were indescribably distorted and malformed, and in some cases their faces and heads had retrograded to the merest mockery of a human countenance. Others again we observed to be lying prone upon the ground as though exhausted from undergoing torture, or because of expending their last remaining energy upon inflicting it.

Benson makes it clear, as do other spirit communicators, that cruelty reigns in some quarters of the afterworld. Further, the impact of a cruel intention in a region devoid of moderating influences, as in the darkest regions of the afterworld, is more stingingly felt than on Earth; for on earth, as Mrs. Owen tells us, "good influences are ever mingling with the bad."

Benson reminds us that "every soul who lives in those awful places once lived upon the earth-plane" where it developed by repetition the habit of cruelty it now continues to inflict on its fellows in the world of spirit. He is also concerned to show how such a dark place came to exist in the first place. It had nothing to do with a supposedly angry God dealing out punishment for sins. Instead, countless generations of human minds have built up over time both the worlds of light and the worlds of darkness:

Beauty of mind and deed can produce nothing but beauty, and hence we have flowers of heavenly beauty, trees and meadows, rivers and streams and seas of pure, glistening , crystal-clear water. . . . But ugliness of mind and deed can produce nothing but ugliness. The seeds of hideousness sown upon the earth-plane will inevitably lead to the reaping of a harvest of hideousness in the spirit world. These dark realms have been built up by the people of the earth-plane, even as they have built up the realms of beauty.

Astral matter responds to mind, either to a conscious wish or an unconscious tendency. Our spirit ancestors have built up for themselves and for us the many realms—light, dark, and all grades between—that we merit by our deeds and habits of mind; and we will extend these realms after we shed our earth bodies.

We see, then, that evil spirits are real and sometimes harm fellow spirits. Can they harm us?

A spirit speaking through Cora Richmond sounds a warning:

In whatever sphere of life, or in whatever state, morally or spiritually, you may be, you are acted upon continually by spiritual powers, for good of ill, for your elevation or depression. These spiritual powers, by continually acting upon your affections and sympathies, move your capabilities to surpassing excellencies, or gravitate with you toward those darksome places and conditions that at some time form the bane of human life.

We saw earlier that earthbound spirits addicted to earth's pleasures can attach themselves to us when we share their addiction. That makes a certain kind of sense. And we've seen, more generally, that spirits who love us visit us unseen, pray for us, and appreciate being remembered by us. We are connected. But to what extent can earthbound spirits—if they can at all—harm the unaddicted?

We should recall the spiritual law that beings in higher worlds can see into lower worlds like our own dense planet, but beings in lower worlds can't see into higher. Zabdiel tells us that

very few [on earth] ... realize in any great degree the magnitude of the forces which are ambient around men as they go about their business day by day. These forces are real, nevertheless, and close at hand. Nay, they mingle with your own endeavors, whether you will or no. And these powers are not all good, but some are malicious, and some betweenwise, and neither definitely good nor bad.

Telesforo, a teacher at the Brazilian spirit colony known as Nosso Lar (Portuguese for "Our Home"), delivered a similar message to a class of novice spirits training to communicate with their "incarnate brothers and sisters." His lecture is reproduced by the spirit Andre Luiz. Telesforo tells the class that as incarnate humans carve out more physical comfort and leisure, they neglect their spirits. As a result, "they do not know themselves," and that ignorance attracts spirits of the wrong kind:

... we are now witnessing individuals being overwhelmed with serious problems not only due to their own deficiencies but also due to their close psychic proximity to the vibratory sphere of the millions of discarnates who cling to the planet's surface, anxious to renew the existence they formerly held in disdain and without the slightest concern for the designs of the Eternal One.

Judge Hatch gives several cautionary examples of how these spirits entangle themselves in our lives:

> When man is excited, exalted, or in any way intensified in his emotional life, the spirits draw near to him. That is how conception is possible; that is the secret of inspiration; that is why anger grows with what it feeds upon. . . . When you lose your temper, you lose a great deal, among other things the control of yourself, and it is barely possible that another entity may momentarily assume control of you.

> This subjective [spirit] world, as I have called it, has its share of inimical spirits. They love to stir up strife, both here and on earth. They enjoy the excitement of anger in others; they are thrilled by the poison of hatred. As certain men revel in morphine, so they revel in all inharmonious passion.

> Do you see the point and the danger? A small seed of anger in your heart they feed and inflame by the hatred in their own. It is not necessarily hatred of you as an individual; often they have no personal interest in you; but for the purpose of gratifying their hostile passion they will attach themselves to you temporarily. . . .

> A man who has the habit of anger, even of fault-finding, is certain to be surrounded by antagonistic spirits. I have seen a score of them around a man, thrilling him with their own malignant magnetism, stirring him up again when by reaction he would have cooled down. . . .

> The same law applies to other unlovely passions, those of lust and avarice. Beware of lust, beware of all sex attraction into which no spiritual or heart element enters. I have seen things that I would not wish to record, either through your hand or any other.

> Let us take a case of avarice. I have seen a miser counting over his gold, have seen the rapacious eyes of spirits which enjoyed the gold through him. . . . Certain spirits love gold, even as a miser loves it, and with the same acquisitive, astringent passion.

Alfredo, a saintly "admininstrator" at one of Nosso Lar's many rescue outposts during World War II, shows us another way that spirits can attack us—not while we're on Earth, but as we're leaving it. His outpost nurses thousands of spirits violently torn from their bodies, and they need direction and protection as they move through the mists that separate earth from light-filled spirit colonies like Nosso Lar. (They end up in Nosso Lar, which hovers over Rio de Janeiro, because European colonies are overflowing with war casualties.) Alfredo tells Luiz, "Our outpost has been placed here like a 'sheep amidst the wolves,' and although it is not our job to exterminate wild beasts [evil spirits], we must nevertheless defend the work of the good against unwarranted attacks."

Some spirit communicators speak of a "battle of wills" between these dark forces stirring up dissension on earth and the opposing forces prompting earth's leaders to live in peace. Alfredo even mentions "projectiles." They are mental, of course. Good spirits with their lighter bodies know how to send out vibrations that "cause the [momentary] illusion of death" on the astral bodies of malevolent beings "less advanced on the path of life." Bear in mind that Alfredo is describing the work of a narrow class of good spirits; few choose to grow their souls so valiantly! But their function is important. "There is a Satanic adversary, elusive yet real," writes Charles Fryer's father, "and he is fighting a losing battle with his Creator, but the war will be a long one, we think . . ." But projectiles? They almost defy belief. Yet the most respected of all spirit communicators mentions them too. Frederic Myers tells us through Geraldine Cummins that thoughts of hate projected from an old enemy on the same spirit plane can produce intense pain and must be guarded against. Astral bodies can't be killed, but they can be assaulted and, to a certain extent, rearranged—at least temporarily.

Is there any hope for these "Satanic" adversaries? Are they lost forever? We know they are free to resist good for as long as they like, and some of them tell us they actually prefer the darkness over the light. But their story doesn't end so bleakly. Monsignor Benson tells us why:

> Every soul who dwells in these dreadful dark realms has the power within himself to rise up out of the foulness into the light. He must make the individual effort himself, he must work out his own redemption. . . . But the golden opportunity of spiritual reclamation is ready and waiting. He has but to show an earnest desire to move himself one fraction of an inch towards the realms of light that are above him, and he will find a host of unknown friends who will help him towards that heritage which is his due, but which in his folly he cast aside.

But why all this eagerness to help those least deserving? Zabdiel tells us:

> And what, then, of those spheres where they who do not love good and beauty dwell? Well, we are also in touch with those, and the help sent there is as readily sent as to the earth sphere; for those realms of darkness are but further removed, and not disconnected, from us. Those who are there are learning their lesson as are you in your earth sphere, but theirs is more dim then yours—no more than this. For still are they sons and daughters of the One All Father, and so our brothers and sisters too.

Nevertheless, the spirit world has extremes of evil just as it has extremes of good. "We once saw a man," says Charles Fryer's father, "whose life was so wicked on earth that he was compelled, not by divine decree but by the operation of his own depraved will, to turn himself into a snake [in appearance]." Another of Andre Luiz's spirit friends, Aniceto, a spirit instructor, offers some helpful advice when encountering such a fiend: pray. Prayer frightens and disconcerts such beings. "Those who pray bear an impenetrable armor." That goes for Earth too. "Every time someone prays in a home, there is a marked improvement in its ambience," and that ambience is a deterrent to vagabond spirits seeking entry: "The home that cultivates prayer becomes a fortress."

Our old friend William James has a view of evil that differs from what we've seen so far—differs so radically that I hardly know how to introduce it. Let's consider it a footnote worth pondering:

> On earth few men are of evil intent. Most crimes are committed by those "out to right a wrong," and are the result of tangled thoughts and emotions that strangle a man's knowledge of himself and others, so that he acts out of ignorance or is driven by a passion that is the only one he allows himself to feel. . . . Few men commit an act called evil for evil's sake . . . unless they confuse evil with good or justify it as the means to a good end. So in death also, there are no "evil" men, and since understanding is clarified, there is no need for mean acts [against them].

18

Reincarnation

In her communication titled *Testimony of Light*, Frances Banks, the Christian nun in earth life, summarizes her afterlife religion under three headings: (1) facing up to her defects and aspiring to correct them, (2) serving and helping others every chance she has, and (3) aspiring to higher states. Reincarnation stands out prominently in her book. It's a key belief that helps make possible each of the three. It stands out in many other spirit communications as well, in fact the majority of accounts that have reached us over the last hundred years. Let's see how the spirits speak of it. Banks writes:

> It is only logical to assume that we take up, as it were, where we left off in a previous trial of strength and weakness. This presupposes a chain of lives, of experiences ... the soul needs to "project" some part of itself back into the denser environment of earth in repeated attempts to master the trials and stresses of those vibrations.

But what's so special about a "denser environment"? AD Mattson explains:

> It's an interesting fact that most persons grow faster spiritually while incarnate. The incarnate energy is denser. That makes it more possible for you, while embodied in flesh on earth, to take hold of a particular problem area and shape it into a more constructive pattern. Your period of incarnation on the physical plane is thus a very important

period of education . . . so most souls do desire to return for a series of incarnations.

What Mattson is saying is that you have to work harder on earth than on the astral planes. Take golf as an example. It takes years to perfect a swing, and once you hit the ball there is nothing you can do to guide it to the target. Golfing on the astral plane would be much easier, indeed so easy that it wouldn't be fun. You could quickly learn to guide the ball to its target with your mind! Or consider the peasant hoeing his patch of cassava. This is hard work and requires dedication to the task. But on the astral there is no need to eat in order to live. Or take the case of the human brain. All of us know what a balky instrument it is. It gets tired, forgets, struggles to understand. Almost all accounts reaching us from the afterlife mention the increased power and quickness of the mind. The less dense astral brain penetrates like a laser beam and doesn't easily forget what it learns. All mental work is easier. The upshot of all this is that earth is the perfect venue for optimal character development. The uncompromising grit of earth's matter makes it a great place to learn discipline and self-sacrifice.

Why are the habits of discipline and self-sacrifice so advantageous in the astral? These are the qualities needed for progress upward to higher, more heavenly spheres. They take us to those realms of light described in Chapter 16.

Professor Ian Currie says,

> We are all striving to reach perfection. This can be quick or slow, depending on our life's progress on both sides of the veil, for an unspecified time. In each lifetime we keep trying to improve ourselves, reincarnating over and over again, climbing through the levels and planes during each stay in the spirit world. . . . we are spirit, going into the physical body on the earth plane to make our progress and then return[ing] to spirit and continually recycling.

But reincarnation has many faces, and the above quotations need texturing and filling out. After all, you could learn what they are telling us from earth's own religions—especially Hinduism or Buddhism. One thing you are not likely to learn from our homegrown religions, however, is that many souls reincarnate out of boredom. Judge Hatch explains: "I shall not do . . . as many souls do; they stay out here [in the astral] until they are as tired of this world as they formerly were tired of the earth, and then are driven back half unconsciously by the irresistible force of the tide of rhythm. I want to guide that rhythm." Stagnation, he tells us elsewhere, is eventually unbearable:

> You should get away from the mental habit of regarding your present [earth] life as the only one, [and] get rid of the idea that the life you expect to live on this side, after your death, is to be an endless existence in one state. You could no more endure such an endless existence in the subtle matter [of the astral] than you could endure to live forever in the gross matter in which you are now encased. You would weary of it. You could not support it.

Hatch gives an example of a spirit who eagerly waited for his earth lover to die. When she did, they were reunited and lived in a "state of subjective bliss" that excluded almost every other experience:

> Now they have each other; they are in "the little house" which he built for her with so much pleasure out of the tenuous materials of the tenuous world; they see each other's faces whether they look out or in; they are content; they have nothing more to attain (or so they tell each other), and they consequently sink back into the arms of subjective bliss. . . . They will enjoy it, I fancy, for a long time, living over the past experiences which they have had together and apart. Then some day one or the other of them will become surfeited with too much sweetness; the muscles of his (or her) soul will stretch for want of exercise; he (or she) will give a spiritual yawn, and by the law of reaction, pass out—not to return.

> Where will he (or she) go, you ask? Why, back to the earth, of course!

It's worth noting that Hatch himself is in no hurry to reincarnate. He sees its necessity, but—

> I rather dread to go back into the world, where it will be so dull for me for a long time. Can I exchange this freedom and vivid life for a long period of somnolence, afterwards to suck a bottle and learn the multiplication table and Greek and Latin verbs? I suppose I must— but not yet.

William James is also reluctant:

> I used to wonder at the hidden microscopic life that teemed in a puddle, or imagine the infinite space a pond must have to a tadpole.... So now earth life seems incredibly small in that respect, yet amazingly active, packed with events as a puddle with drops of water, each seemingly separate yet each connected. I wonder that I ever put myself into that context. At the same time, that experience added immeasurably to my existence, but I do not wish to repeat it.

Apart from its desirability, it's no easy thing to reincarnate. If done right, it could take "years of preparation" according to Mattson. If not done right, you might have no say in the matter, not even regarding who your parents are. Mattson devotes a chapter describing the perils of an unguided, unprotected reincarnation. "I think that eventually my own main interest," he says, "is going to be not in helping those who have just left the earth, but in helping those who are going back down to earth."

Motives behind the desire to reincarnate differ. In the example of the two lovers we saw souls who might dwell at their present level for a long time. They don't miss earth, and they show no interest in advancing to higher spheres. But there are other souls here, Judge Hatch tells us, "who are homesick for the earth. They sometimes go back almost at once, which is generally a mistake." Sometimes relatively advanced souls go back. Myers calls these beings "Soul-men" to distinguish them from "Animal-men." Myers says, "Certain Soul-men desire to return to earth, or wish, at any rate, for some planetary existence wherein they may achieve some intellectual triumph, or wherein they may play a notable part in the strife of earthly or planetary life. These, then, become incarnate again." We can imagine Mozart, Churchill, or Einstein—or countless unsung souls tirelessly following their dream. Myers adds that "the majority of Soul-men slough their etheric body and put on a shape which is a degree finer" and never return to the density of earth. Myers himself doesn't expect to.

People often ask how many lives a soul typically lives on earth before permanently moving on. James gives no rule. "Some individuals return to physical life many times. Others live a life or two of great intensity and then follow through with ideas from this end, watching as the physical seeds of that creativity [on earth] sprout, but from a distance." Do adolescent suicides suffer a different fate from others?

Stephen says, "Many of the kids will not come back during the lifetime of their families. . . . It usually takes longer to prepare suicides to return than that. A lot of parents and relatives will meet their children immediately after they themselves die."

What about young children? We already know they go to school and grow up in the astral world. But do they reincarnate? Judge Hatch says: "Children grow up out here, and they may even go on to a sort of old age if that is the expectation of the mind; but the tendency is to keep to the prime, to go forward or back towards the best period, and then to hold that until the irresistible attraction of the earth asserts itself again." He's reminding us that souls who shed the body at a very young age have lived before on Earth and will live there again. He implies that since the purpose of incarnation was defeated by an early death, a return is likely.

Do spirits have anything to tell us about the impact of an abortion on the process of reincarnation? The subject is complex. One of Allan Kardec's unnamed spirits says that the "mother, or anyone else, who takes the life of an unborn child is committing a crime. Why? Because an abortion prevents the soul from undergoing the trial of which the destroyed body was to have been the instrument." But AD Mattson, the Protestant minister and theologian, takes a more nuanced position:

> If a fetus is aborted in the second or third month of pregnancy, it appears that the in-coming soul has not yet drawn close enough to the auric field of the mother to be too adversely affected. Since it may not even be aware of the fact, the disruption is not as drastic as some people believe. However, when you abort a fetus at any point after conception, you are really contravening the creative laws of the universe. You are interrupting a creative process that has been set in motion on many levels. If you destroy a body that could be used for an in-coming soul, that soul is deprived of opportunity, and the mother, also, is often left with a debilitating sense of frustration.

An even more nuanced position is given us by "Seth," a spirit who recalls lives as far back as 350, one of them as a monk:

> The reincarnating personality enters the new fetus according to its own inclinations, desires, and characteristics, with some built-in safeguards. However there is no rule, then, saying that the reincarnating personality must take over the new form prepared for it either at the

point of conception, in the very earliest months of the fetus's growth, or even at the point of birth.

Seth goes on to say that even if the soul enters at the point of conception, "large portions of self-awareness continue to operate in the between-life dimension." According to Mattson and Seth, "murder" would be too harsh a word to apply to an abortion. On the other hand, warnings against the act are stern.

A number of spirits refer to a sex change between lives, and several tie it into homosexuality. Seth explains: "If an individual considers identity strongly in terms of male or female identity, then such a person may refuse to accept the fact of the sexual changes that occur in reincarnational existences. This kind of sexual identification, however, also impedes personality development during physical life." Mattson gets underneath homosexual tendencies and takes a much gentler, more qualified approach:

> Some souls coming into incarnation as women keep in the core of their being a desire for a close, loving, caring relationship with another woman. Their experiences in male/female relationships in other lives may have been hurtful and debasing, producing loneliness and a struggle to be respected as an individual. So now, instinctively fearing roughness and loneliness in this present life, they reach back to imprints of a past incarnation where they experienced happiness with an all-female group . . . and they establish relationships with other women.

> Likewise, some men, because of imprints of past incarnations and the customs of those times, come into incarnation and seek comfort, sustenance, and peace with another like-minded male.

It's noteworthy that these spirits make no mention of the physical brain. Homosexual tendencies—along with all other tendencies we are born with—result from habits built up over previous lives, not from the structure or chemistry of our brains.

It might come as a surprise to learn that reincarnation is not universally acknowledged in the afterworld. Apparently many spirits cling to their old earth ideas with a tenacity that almost defies belief. One of Kardec's spirits explains that some spirits "never give [reincarnation] a thought and—strange as it may seem—know nothing about it. In some cases, they are left in uncertainty about their future as a form of admonition and correction." Judge Hatch concurs: "Most of the men and women here do not know that they have lived many times in flesh. They remember their latest life more or less vividly, but all before that seems like a dream." Thus they are unaware that they are unfinished products and that there is still more work to do. Hatch explains how this odd ignorance comes to be:

> These people here, being in the subjective, reason from the premises already given them during their objective or earth existence. That is why most of those who last lived in the so-called Western lands, where the idea of rhythm or rebirth is unpopular, came out here with the fixed idea that they would not go back into earth life. Hence most of them still reason from that premise.

In other words, since astral matter is so malleable, or "subjective," or maneuverable, spirits often inhabit a world largely built up by their collective unconscious imagination. And that imagination was formed by the mental habits and assumptions of earth. In certain sectors of the afterworld –for example, most Christian sectors—those assumptions contradict reincarnation. On earth, by contrast, you don't always get what your mind assumes to be true; you constantly bump up against a world that is "objective." We see here, incidentally, another instance of why it's so important to descend into flesh.

It would be wrong, as I read the situation, to conclude that these "Westernized" souls never wake up to the fact that they should go back to earth for their own advancement. They will gradually "have presentiments of it," says Kardec's spirit, "in the same way a blind person feels heat when approaching fire." They will adjust. More correctly, they will adjust their beliefs if they have to. The true saints among them will eventually move forward into higher heavens, of course, without needing to reincarnate. But even they would do well to remember their previous lives in order to "see the roads by which [their] souls have come," as Hatch puts it.

Another question that arises—and the most important in my view— is the relation between the soul or "deep self" and the personalities that the soul clothes itself with in repeated lives. The Buddha was especially concerned about this very thing. He concluded that a man in his next life wouldn't be the same as in the present life, even though he inherited that man's karma. But he wouldn't be different either! Neither the one nor the other, he said.

What do the spirits say? The spirit who came through the American medium Suzy Smith and claimed to be William James (though even Smith doubted his true identity) disbelieved in reincarnation. He says, "When one is living a life he is that person, he is not just playing a role or a series of roles; so if he were to go through the lifetimes of a variety of different people, he would end up completely confused about his identity." He then admits that reincarnation does occur in exceptional cases, but that it leads to "their utter bewilderment at the end of their second experience."

A much more common view of the relation between intrinsic being and outer personality comes to us from Seth. After granting that "there are many complicated issues here," he makes a distinction between the "new personality" or "new individual" or "new identity" and the "entire identity." It's the latter that reincarnates. As the new fetus grows, Seth says,

> the self from the previous incarnation must begin to withdraw its hold . . . it does not *become* the new individual. . . . The new individual has a deeply buried memory of its past lives, but the personal consciousness of the last reincarnated self must not be superimposed upon this new identity. The new personality . . . is very much its own self.

In this way the confusion referred to above is circumvented.

Another way to make sense of the relation between a being's underlying identity and that identity's several incarnations comes from the "Group Soul" concept. Many spirits, we are told, are members of large spirit families, or "Group Souls," that await them when they pass. They feel as if they have come home when they are received by the familiar Group. You might recall that Frances Banks tells us that souls in a Group are "part of ourselves. Their connection with us is deeper and far more permanent than mere earth contacts could make it."

What this has to do with reincarnation is best told by Frederic Myers. "I shall not live again on earth," he declares,

> but a new soul, one who will join our group, will shortly enter into the pattern or karma I have woven for him on earth. . . . You may say to me that, for the Soul-man, one earth life is not enough. But, as we evolve here, we enter into those memories and experiences of other

lives that are to be found in the existence of the souls that preceded us, and are of the group.

Myers is saying, to take an example, that Einstein arrived at his genius not from the hard work he did in a previous life, but from the work that other members of his Group did when they were incarnate. By a kind of osmosis their gifts were transferred to his psyche, and the very reason for the Group's existence—to produce a magnificent scientific genius for the greater good of Earth—was realized in the life of Einstein. Einstein was their gift to the material world they sought to serve. This is a good example, incidentally, of afterlife "religion" at its best, a religion of service in action.

If this theory were true universally—if all of us owed our talents and basic disposition to kindred souls in our Group—reincarnation would be a false teaching. But Myers does not claim this. The ordinary person (or Animal-man), he explains, "longs for a new life" on earth:

> So he goes downwards; but he descends in order to rise. His experiences in the dream of the earth personality rouse the higher part of the self in him. During his next incarnation he will probably either enter into the state of the Soul-man, or he will at least be less of an animal, and will seek an existence and follow a life of a higher order than the one he led when previously lodged in the flesh.

So there you have it: the usual teaching.

But it is a teaching full of mystery, and no one puts it better than the advanced spirit known as Imperator:

> There are still mysteries . . . into which it is not well that man should penetrate. One of such mysteries is the ultimate development and destiny of spirits. Whether in the eternal counsels of the Supreme it may be deemed well that a particular spirit should or should not be again incarnated in a material form is a question that none [at your level] can know, not even the spirit's own guides. What is wise and well will be done.

Mystery or not, all spirits leave us with the teaching that what we do while incarnate is of the utmost importance. Myers sums up the purpose of all incarnation, whether of the grosser form we are living through now on Earth, or the subtler form that awaits us after death, in these words:

> The reason, therefore, for the universe and for all appearances, for even the little mundane joys and sorrows of human beings, is to be found in the term "evolution of spirit," the need for complete fulfillment which can be obtained through limitation, through the expression of the spirit in form. For only through that expression can spirit grow, developing from the embryo, only through manifestation in appearance can spirit obtain fulfillment. For this purpose were we born, for this purpose we enter and pass through myriad worlds or states, and always the material universe is growing, expanding, giving fuller and fuller expression to mind.... The myriad thoughts of God, those spirits which inform with life all material forms, are the lowest manifestation of God, and must thus learn to become God-like—to become an effective part of the Whole.

Conclusion

I owe much to our spirit friends; they, more than any other source, have helped me develop my own worldview. What I termed their "meta-religion" has become my personal religion. I find myself wondering how many of you can relate to it, even partially.

What follows are contrasts between the meta-religion of our spirit friends and the religions of our own world. I think you will see how our religions suffer by comparison.

1. Earth's religions usually visualize heaven as a place of joyful rest. But what does one do with all the time at one's disposal? Just rest? Are there no more challenges, no further prizes to be won?

Christianity and Islam aren't the only religions to place an emphasis on the blissful restfulness of the afterlife. Buddhism in its own way leaves the same impression. The most blissful state open to mortals after death is the "realm of the gods" where those with good karma now reside. Nothing they do there creates further merit or demerit. They simply enjoy the fruits of their karma before it runs out and they face rebirth in a less blissful state. The same goes for those beings dwelling in hell or as an animal or as an earthbound spirit. Nothing they do in these states can deliver them from their woe. Many Hindus have a similar view of the state between incarnations: you enjoy or suffer the fruits of your karma until your soul is reborn again as a human. Only then can you advance.

But our spirit friends unanimously place great value on what we do *between earth lives*. It too provides a venue for growing our soul.

All states do. The meta-religion of our spirit friends is what guides and stimulates souls in the afterworld to take the high road. But the will is always free, and the low road, the road of sloth and selfishness, is there for the taking. Karma is always in play. Living in an environment where the stakes are always high is much more attractive to me than one where there are prolonged time-outs. Making allowances for weakness in so radical a fashion diminishes the dignity and efficiency of the soul-making project.

2. In all my research into the afterlife I've never come across an account of an attempted conversion from one of earth's religions to another. That's because it becomes quickly clear to spirits living in the regions of light that *character*, not belief, governs one's place in the heavens.

The contemporary Christian writer Marcus Borg thinks that emphasizing belief over character impoverishes Christianity: "This preoccupation with 'believing' and 'beliefs' has a crucially important effect: it turns Christian faith into a 'head matter.' Faith becomes primarily a matter of *the beliefs in your head*—of whether you believe the right set of claims to be true." Every spirit writer I've read makes the same complaint against a head-based religion. As for me, I wonder how we ever came to the point where beliefs became more important than the deeds we do and the character we form.

3. Christianity's theologians have for centuries defined heaven as seeing God face to face, sometimes called the "beatific vision." We are sometimes left with the impression that the company of heaven—all her saints—do little else but worship God in this fashion. Our spirit friends have much to say about worship. First, they don't claim to "see God," as if God had a face and was situated in space, and their lives are full of every other kind of activity. But there *are* times for worship for those so inclined.

We can expect ecstatic moments during communal worship on the Other Side. "Here our ceremonies," Frances Banks says, "spring from an innate oneness with the Source of all Life, an eagerness to participate, a welling upwards of the Life Force in us so as to initiate a mingling with one another as well as with the Greater Forces." Clearly worship Over There, if Banks is an authentic witness, as I believe she is, is on a far grander scale than here.

4. "God" is a troublesome word for many of us. What does the God of our spirit friends look like? First—and this might surprise you at first glance—their God is personal, not an It. But not personal in the fallible, limited way we are, not categorizable by a Myers-Briggs personality test or how S/He would treat a waitress, but having a unique intellectual and emotional structure infinitely beyond ours. Not an impersonal mystical power like the "Force" served by Jedi warriors, but a matchless Being who knows us, values us, even loves us—loves us because we are that Being's creations. More than that, because this Being ensouls us. We are not related to the Divine as pottery to the potter, but as child to parent. At our core we are made of the very stuff of the Divine; we are tiny atoms of light one and the same with the Light itself. Therefore it's natural, even inevitable, for the Divine to watch us, follow us, expect great things of us, forgive us when we fall short, preserve us beyond death, keep the soul-making adventure going. Why? Because the Divine is hidden in our depths—the permanent "Guest," in the words of Kabir—and wants nothing more than to bring us into the Kingdom of Spirit as his/her immortal children, if only we would agree to come.

In my mid-twenties I lost my faith. I was miserable at the prospect of a world without meaning followed by a death I'd never wake up from. "A flash of light between two eternities of darkness," as the philosopher Unamuno put it—that's all we amounted to. I had escaped the cramping theology I grew up with, but what I stepped into was even worse. After much soul-searching and study, especially after discovering the riches of spirit literature, I found something far superior to both: a joyous, compassionate, loving, powerful, boundless, light-filled Reality at the hub of the universe with an outreach that extended to the epicenter of my soul, a Being that would resonate with a Buddhist as well as a Christian. A God roomy enough even for an atheist.

5. The nature of Jesus the Christ is another trouble spot that our spirit friends bring light to. The Jesus they describe—and recall that most of them were Christians in earth life—is not some unique supernatural eruption of Godhead onto the planet, but a prototype of what we all are. Whenever we are ready, we can nurse along the divine seed in our depths. Jesus, and other rare souls like him, most of them unknown to history, allowed this seed to blossom to an utterly extraordinary degree. His remarkable spiritual achievements and grisly death led to his being divinized by his followers, a process repeated many

times in the world's history. Overlooked by his disciples at first was the possibility that what Jesus achieved they could too. And indeed many of them would go on to achieve great things against terrible odds in imitation of their master.

The divinization of Jesus, officially promulgated at the Council of Nicea in 325, was unfair to him. That a mere man could sacrifice so much is astonishing. That God could do it is much less so. Spirit teaching underscores Jesus's achievement, then holds it out to us as a model to be followed.

6. As we know by now, our spirit friends affirm with utmost confidence, from direct experience, and with one voice that perfect justice reigns on the Other Side. Justice that sees through all camouflages, has all the facts, and works without fail is the "law of the land." Many spirits suffered unjustly on Earth, some acutely, under legal systems which could not, even if uncorrupted, see very far into the human heart and properly weigh its motivations. Others profited unfairly under the same inevitable sloppiness of these systems. Either way, the wheels of a true justice, the spirits tell us, begin to turn when death finally comes. And they continue to turn long after death. All effort, all loving service in the heaven worlds is noted, and promotion to higher states rests on these efforts. So does the passage back into flesh. What we call the law of karma is a universal cosmic principle. I long for this kind of world. I think we all do.

7. The habit of giving service while on earth is the best preparation for eternity—or a better life next time round. Our spirit friends see this with a clarity that we lack. They fear we are going to die leaving behind little more than a legacy of selfishness. Many of them left little more themselves, and they don't want us to make the same mistake. They know, as we do not, how costly that can be. Further, as we've already seen, the ideal of service doesn't stop at death. We see many examples of spirits working in the "trenches" of the Shadowlands to bring relief and instruction to those oppressed by their environment. And they counsel us earthlings via telepathy and oppose evil spirits bent on harming us. What motivates all this apparent altruism? Is it compassion and love? Or is it the hope of reward and advancement? As I read it, it's a combination of both. As well it should be.

Either way, the spirits are reinforcing what most of earth's religions have been telling us all along. What makes them different is the vivid protrayals of the consequences of vice and the rewards of virtue. By contrast, earth's visions of an otherworldly heaven and hell are mainly guesswork and are recognized as such. Thus they seldom incite us to virtuous behavior. We need incentive systems we can take seriously, ways of seeing our world that will inspire generosity, unselfish service, and forgiveness. The spirits give us this.

8. It would be a horrible thing if we all received the same "reward" at death. We abhor the idea of Hitler rubbing shoulders with Mother Teresa or even with our comparatively lowly selves. This gut reaction, this flinching at the very thought, doesn't arise from selfishness or a sense that we are among the spiritual elite. It arises because our hearts crave justice. Therefore we expect and hope that people who create hell for others will have to experience it for themselves. And that is exactly what happens according to the spirits.

On the other hand, the doctrine that hell is a cosmic ghetto where sinners are herded against their wills for all eternity, with no possibility of reform or release, a typical cachet of certain religions, is equally abhorrent to justice-loving souls. Our spirit friends tell us that neither of these perversions of justice is a hallmark of the afterworld. Heaven and hell there are, along with every conceivable grade of each, as well as a great variety of purgatories in between, but the extremes we find in earth's theologies find no match in reality.

9. I might lose most of you here, but I welcome the warnings about evil spirits working their mischief on our plane. The highly evolved spirit Imperator warns us not to play into the hands of "lower spirits who hover nearest earth, and who are but too ready to rush in and mar our plans, and ruin our work for souls." He refers to a "direct antagonism between them and us, between the work which is for man's development and instruction, and their efforts to retard and thwart it."

Why do educated people scoff at the thought of such spiritual warfare? It goes on all around us, and inside us, on earth among our embodied selves, so why should it cease just because we die? One lesson we should have learned by now: God, or the Great Spirit, or the Divine, or whatever name you want to give the Creator, doesn't interfere in our problems. If he did, then we would be feeble pawns under his control. On the other hand, we are not left without protection against all this invisible evil, but we must grasp our condition and take steps to shield ourselves from it. Imperator says, "Praise, which attunes the soul to God, and prayer, which moves the spirit agencies—these are engines ever ready to man's service." But we must actively seek this help—seek it in the same way we would seek help on earth from our friends or family. And if we don't, then we are likely to be left to our own devices.

If our spirit friends are correct, then our religions for the most part greatly underestimate the power of evil around us and the help available from our spirit friends to vanquish it. Once again, we must look to heaven for guidance. When we do, then we'll see that Jesus knew exactly what he was doing when he "cast out demons." As does the Chinese Daoist priest in China or the Hindu baba in India whose life's calling is to do the same for a non-Christian culture.

10. Are we young souls with no previous histories, or old souls with rich, checkered histories drawn from several or many incarnations? I don't know for sure, but the spirits generally favor the old-soul theory. It seems likely to me that the Creator thinks we're worth salvaging–over and over. If so, the universe, in addition to being an arena where ultimate justice is meted out through character karma, takes on a merciful hue.

However, there is also a consensus among spirits that souls, once sufficiently progressed, will not need to return to earth. So the reincarnational process will have been concluded for many spirits, and they will go forward into immortality. We also know that spirits tend to cluster with their own kind when they first come over following death. Southern Baptist Christians will lovingly receive those who think like they do, and Hindus of the Dvaita school of Vedanta will find a warm reception when they die from fellow Dvaitins. The Christians will deny what the Hindus affirm. So it's not surprising that there should be inconsistency in the spirit communications we receive.

The notion that souls cluster together with others of like mind and background following death strikes me as likely, and I've found nothing like it in the teachings of the world's religions. Also helpful is the spirits' explanation of why certain spirit clusters would affirm the teaching of rebirth while others would not. In general I find some of my most vexing metaphysical questions answered by spirits—the same questions that many of our world's foremost philosophers and theologians don't even allow themselves to ask.

11. Monsignor Benson describes the most evolved being he has ever met as "the merriest soul in the whole of the spirit realms." Charles

Fryer's father tells how he and his companions "often talk about our various activities, and there is much merriment at times, for we are not gloomy here, and laughter is the rule when someone tells us something that is incongruous or funny." I find no hint of merriment or laughter in any of the world's scriptures. The fact that our spirit friends have a sense of humor is a matter for rejoicing!

12. Valuing what is right in front of our face is an easy thing. For us the greater challenge is to value the world we will soon enter. Most of us would value that world more if we had a clearer idea of what it was. Thanks to the spirits, we've examined it closely here; we've seen it in living color and in great detail. We've seen that the religion of heaven, what we've called the meta-religion of the afterlife, asks much of spirits and that those who embrace its challenges advance to higher realms of joy and responsibility. Loving service comes easier over there than here because there is much less grinding toil, but disappointments can be keenly felt. The joy that we associate with heaven is commensurate with the help we lovingly give to those who need it.

It would be pretentious and elitist to blame our religions for their failures in perspective. After all, we are the creators of these religions, and what should we expect from our divine souls as they partner with our dense brains in the dance of life on a physical planet? If it weren't for our religions, we wouldn't be as free from delusion and distortion as we are.

But our religions are attached to their doctrines with Gorilla Glue, and needed change comes centuries late, if at all. Of all the religions I've studied, only Mormonism teaches "progressive revelation": Mormons believe that God reveals new truth or even corrects false teaching from time to time through successive "Presidents" of the Mormon faith. While most Biblical Christians see this doctrine as a fatal weakness, I see it as a strength.

If the idea of progressive revelation were accepted more widely, then more of us would allow ourselves to be nourished by the teachings of our spirit friends. The world's collective IQ would rise and its blood pressure drop. There would be less atheism and fewer wars. Crime rates would fall, and the modern addiction to money and fame would be a cause for shame.

The astral world described by our spirit friends is an incredibly beautiful and interesting place not so different from our own earth; we have every reason to look forward to it. It's different enough to inspire awe and amazement, but "homey" enough to allow us to relax in the company of those who love us. The "communion of saints" mentioned in the Nicene Creed is exactly what our spirit friends are describing, but in language less pious.

The "religion from heaven" given us by our spirit friends is, in my view, much superior to the ones we humans have cobbled together over the centuries. I'm tempted to predict that earth's future religions will gradually tend to resemble it—as dusty towns with no landscaping gradually turn greener as their citizens travel to nearby cities where trees have been planted down every median. It takes time, but in the long run, the very long run, we humans tend to change for the better. Our views of the afterlife, of heaven and hell, will be, let us hope, no exception.

There are few scholars in the world who have given as much time and thought to the afterlife as I, but I expect to be amazed when I open my eyes on the spectacle before me when I pass. I am well aware that the words reaching us from spirits are only feeble symbols of the thing itself, and that this entire book can be seen as a map. About maps, Aldous Huxley had this to say: "Maps are symbols, and even the best of them are inaccurate and imperfect symbols. But to anyone who really wants to reach a given destination, a map is indispensably useful as indicating the direction in which the traveler should set out and the roads which he must take." I think that all of us, especially including myself, will see things following death in ways we never dreamed of, and that we'll chuckle at our conceits.

Appendix

Judaism in the Afterlife

You might have noticed that all but one of our spirit friends lived in the Western hemisphere before they died. Moreover, most were Christians in earth life, and their background influenced their postmortem experiences—some more, some less. The question naturally arises: What about Jews? Don't Jewish spirits speak to us from the afterworld?

I haven't come across any so far who identify themselves as Jewish. But bear in mind that for every Jew on earth, there are more than 150 Christians. Also remember that not all spirits identify themselves as having been members of an earth religion. Nevertheless, it would be most instructive to come across a Jewish communicator.

But we do have the next best thing: a Jew who was regressed and remembers her experiences in the afterlife. Her name today is Abbye Silverstein, and her story is told in Rabbi Yonassan Gershom's book *From Ashes to Healing: Mystical Encounters with the Holocaust.* Under hypnosis she saw her life unfold as a Jewish woman named Anna; her husband is named Richard. She describes both Richard and herself in the third person, as "they." Both died in a car crash in France while trying to escape the Nazis. Then—

> In the spirit world, they were welcomed by a guard standing beside a large door. He walked them to a reception table in the Great Hall. A woman there welcomed them and explained that they were going to continue their lives in this world now. She told them that they were in training to help others. They had been spared the horrors of the Holocaust in order to be of service to the victims. They were sent to heavenly classes, where

they studied with the great Jewish masters about religion, philosophy, psychology, and the psychic healing of the soul.

Anna's first assignment in the spirit world was as an intake worker. On the earth below, the Jews were being exterminated, and souls were entering the in-between world at a very rapid rate. She was placed in the Great Hall, which was like the "Ellis Island" of Heaven, run by the "United Jewish Appeal" of the in-between world. The Jewish souls came in droves, with their astral bodies crippled and mangled with torture, degraded, and stripped of their dignity.

As an intake worker, Anna took their vital statistics for the Akashic Record: name, place of birth, residence, occupation, family history, manner of death, etc. Soon she met her mother, father, sister, and best friend as they stood in line to check in. They had died in the Holocaust. Like the rest of the Jews, they were sent to a section of the afterworld that was designated "for Jews only"—not to segregate them, but to provide a place where their wounded spirits could heal in an atmosphere of safety.

This Jewish part of Heaven was divided into countries, cities, villages, and towns, which paralleled their homes on earth. Bulletin boards were created according to geographical regions, which posted messages for the incoming souls to find their relatives. Maps and signposts aided them in going home. Everything that had been left behind on the material plane was re-created in the spirit world in order to help these severely wounded souls make the transition toward reincarnating as the Baby Boom generation. There was a great deal of work to do in a very short period of time.

Anna was happy in the in-between world, and her life was very productive. She was "promoted" several times, until she was the supervisor of a type of healing center. As such, she attended a council of healing center administrators, to share ideas for healing and helping those Holocaust souls make the transition.

When the war ended in 1945, the Jewish section was opened up, and people were able to travel to other parts of the in-between world. Anna's husband, Richard, was preparing to reincarnate again, to be among the first wave of Baby Boomers. Anna, on the other hand, did not want to leave. . . .

In such cases as these there is the ever present chance of the patient's imagination subconsciously inventing stories to please her therapist. We know this often happens in regression therapy, but there is also much evidence to suggest that some memories brought to light during hypnosis are real.

Putting this question aside, what stands out for me is the consistency of this narrative with the many accounts we've seen from non-Jewish sources. In this single brief story we see the same emphasis on familiar landscapes and cityscapes, on damage done to the astral bodies of those who have been abused (see Chapter 15), on the almost universal need of healing, on "training to help others" by master teachers, on assigned jobs to perform, on "promotion" for generous service, on meeting loved ones, on clustering with one's cultural group, on the gradual opening up and travel to "other parts of the in-between world," and on reincarnation. It all sounds so familiar, but with a Yiddish twang.

If this woman's account is true, we have all the more reason to rejoice. Ethnic customs are preserved for as long as they are treasured, but there is a tendency to outgrow them in favor of a common culture unique to the heaven worlds. And for those attracted to the traditions and habits of earth, reincarnation is a ready vehicle.

Key References

Barker, Elsa (1995). *Letters from the Afterlife.* Hillsboro, Oregon: Beyond Words.

Borgia, Anthony (no date). *Life in the World Unseen.* San Francisco: H. G. White.

Chism, Stephen (2005). *The Afterlife of Leslie Stringfellow.* Fayetteville, Arkansas: Fullcourte

Crookall, Robert. (1961). *The Supreme Adventure.* Cambridge, England: James Clarke.

Cummins, Geraldine (1955). *The Road to Immortality.* London: Aquarian Press.

Cummins, Geraldine. (1965). *Swan on a Black Sea.* London: Routledge and Kegan Paul.

Fryer, Charles. (1982). *A Hand in Dialogue. Cambridge,* England: James Clarke.

Greaves, Helen (1977). *Testimony of Light.* Saffron Walden, England: C. W. Daniel.

Johnson, Raynor. (1964). *The Light and the Gate.* London: Hodder and Stoughton.

Kardec, Allan. (2003). *The Spirits' Book*. Philadelphia: Allan Kardec Educational Society.

Lees, Robert J. (1898). *Through the Mists*. London: Rider.

Lodge, Oliver. (1915). *Raymond or Life and Death*. New York: George H. Doran.

Moses, W. Stainton (1976). *Spirit Teachings*. New York: Arno Press.

Ortzen, Tony., ed. (1986). *Silver Birch Companion*. London: Psychic Press.

Owen, G. Vale. (2007). *The Life Beyond the Veil*. Grande Prairie, Alberta, Canada: Red Pill Press.

Puryear, Anne. (1993). *Stephen Lives!* Scottsdale, Arizona: New Paradigm.

Richmond, Cora. (1878). *Is Materialization True?* Boston: Colby & Rich.

Roberts, Jane. (1972). *Seth Speaks*. Englewood Cliffs, New Jersey: Prentice-Hall.

Roberts, Jane. (1978). *The Afterdeath Journal of an American Philosopher*. Englewood Cliffs, NJ: Prentice-Hall.

Stead, W. T. (1971). *The Blue Island*, 3rd ed. Washington, D.C.: ESPress.

Swedenborg, Emanuel. (1976). *Heaven and Hell*. New York: Pillar Books.

Tappan (Richmond), Cora. (1876). *Experiences of Judge J. W. Edmonds in Spirit Life*. Chicago: A.M. Griffen.

Taylor, R. Mattson (1980). *Witness from Beyond*. South Portland, Maine: Foreword Press.

Taylor, R. Mattson (1999). *Evidence from Beyond*. Brooklyn, NY: Brett Books.

Thomas, Drayton. (no date). *Beyond Life's Sunset*. London: Psychic Press.

Thomas, Drayton. (no date). *In the Dawn Beyond Death*. London: Lectures Universal.

White, Stewart. (1940). *The Unobstructed Universe*. New York: E. P. Dutton.

Williams, Bill. (2006). *Life in the Spirit World*. Victoria, B.C., Canada: Trafford.

Xavier, Francisco. (2006). *Nosso Lar*. Brasilia, Brazil: International Spiritist Council.

Xavier, Francisco. (2008). *The Messengers*. Brasilia, Brazil: International Spiritist Council.

Yogananda, Paramahansa. (1973). *Autobiography of a Yogi*. Los Angeles: Self- Realization Fellowship.

Acknowledgements

For permission to use selections throughout this book, grateful acknowledgement and thanks are extended to the following authors and publishers.

From the book *Seth Speaks*. Copyright © 1972 by Jane Roberts. Reprinted with permission of New World Library, Novato, CA.

Stephen Chism, *The Afterlife of Leslie Stringfellow* (Fayetteville, Arkansas: Fullcourte Press, 2005)

Anne Puryear, *Stephen Lives!* (Scottsdale, Arizona: New Paradigm Press, 1992)

Helen Greaves, *Testimony of Light* (London: Rider/Random House, 2005)

Tony Orzen, ed., & Maurice Barbanell, *Silver Birch Companion* (London: Psychic Press, 1986)

Charles Fryer, *A Hand in Dialogue* (Cambridge: James Clarke, 1982)

Jane Roberts, *The Afterdeath Journal of an American Philosopher* (New Awareness Network, 2001)

I especially want to thank two people who have made this book possible. Michael Tymn, who might have a more encyclopedic knowledge of spirit sources than anyone else alive, has put me in contact with some of those sources that were critical to the evolution of this book. And Jon Beecher, publisher of White Crow Books, a unique emporium of books on spirit, has shown great faith in this project from the start and patiently endured more than a few "final" drafts on the way to production.

INDEX

V

Vedanta, 142
Venue for growing our soul, 137
Vibration, 14, 91, 107
Vietnam, 90
Visit, 18, 53, 55, 80, 86, 97, 121, 123

W

Wesley, John, 43
White, Betty, 29-30, 44, 71, 77-78,
    83, 110, 149, 151, 154
Wilde, Oscar, 95
Wolpe, Rabbi David, 21

Worship, 107, 109-115, 138

X

Xavier, Chico, 105, 151

Y

Yiddish twang, 147
Yogananda, Paramahamsa, 43, 151
Yukteswar, 43

Z

Zabdiel, 19, 30, 34, 39, 45, 65, 67, 84,
    87, 98, 103, 113, 123, 126

Paperbacks also available from
White Crow Books

Elsa Barker—*Letters from
a Living Dead Man*
ISBN 978-1-907355-83-7

Elsa Barker—*War Letters from
the Living Dead Man*
ISBN 978-1-907355-85-1

Elsa Barker—*Last Letters from
the Living Dead Man*
ISBN 978-1-907355-87-5

Richard Maurice Bucke—
Cosmic Consciousness
ISBN 978-1-907355-10-3

Arthur Conan Doyle—
The Edge of the Unknown
ISBN 978-1-907355-14-1

Arthur Conan Doyle—
The New Revelation
ISBN 978-1-907355-12-7

Arthur Conan Doyle—
The Vital Message
ISBN 978-1-907355-13-4

Arthur Conan Doyle with
Simon Parke—*Conversations
with Arthur Conan Doyle*
ISBN 978-1-907355-80-6

Meister Eckhart with Simon Parke—
Conversations with Meister Eckhart
ISBN 978-1-907355-18-9

D. D. Home—*Incidents in my Life Part 1*
ISBN 978-1-907355-15-8

Mme. Dunglas Home; edited,
with an Introduction, by Sir
Arthur Conan Doyle—*D. D.
Home: His Life and Mission*
ISBN 978-1-907355-16-5

Edward C. Randall—
Frontiers of the Afterlife
ISBN 978-1-907355-30-1

Rebecca Ruter Springer—
Intra Muros: My Dream of Heaven
ISBN 978-1-907355-11-0

Leo Tolstoy, edited by Simon
Parke—*Forbidden Words*
ISBN 978-1-907355-00-4

Leo Tolstoy—*A Confession*
ISBN 978-1-907355-24-0

Leo Tolstoy—*The Gospel in Brief*
ISBN 978-1-907355-22-6

Leo Tolstoy—*The Kingdom
of God is Within You*
ISBN 978-1-907355-27-1

Leo Tolstoy—*My Religion:
What I Believe*
ISBN 978-1-907355-23-3

Leo Tolstoy—*On Life*
ISBN 978-1-907355-91-2

Leo Tolstoy—*Twenty-three Tales*
ISBN 978-1-907355-29-5

Leo Tolstoy—*What is Religion
and other writings*
ISBN 978-1-907355-28-8

Leo Tolstoy—*Work While
Ye Have the Light*
ISBN 978-1-907355-26-4

Leo Tolstoy—*The Death of Ivan Ilyich*
ISBN 978-1-907661-10-5

Leo Tolstoy—*Resurrection*
ISBN 978-1-907661-09-9

Leo Tolstoy with Simon Parke—
Conversations with Tolstoy
ISBN 978-1-907355-25-7

Howard Williams with an Introduction
by Leo Tolstoy—*The Ethics of Diet:
An Anthology of Vegetarian Thought*
ISBN 978-1-907355-21-9

Vincent Van Gogh with Simon
Parke—*Conversations with Van Gogh*
ISBN 978-1-907355-95-0

Wolfgang Amadeus Mozart with Simon
Parke—*Conversations with Mozart*
ISBN 978-1-907661-38-9

Jesus of Nazareth with Simon Parke—
Conversations with Jesus of Nazareth
ISBN 978-1-907661-41-9

Thomas à Kempis with Simon
Parke—*The Imitation of Christ*
ISBN 978-1-907661-58-7

Julian of Norwich with Simon
Parke—*Revelations of Divine Love*
ISBN 978-1-907661-88-4

Allan Kardec—*The Spirits Book*
ISBN 978-1-907355-98-1

Allan Kardec—*The Book on Mediums*
ISBN 978-1-907661-75-4

Emanuel Swedenborg—*Heaven and Hell*
ISBN 978-1-907661-55-6

P.D. Ouspensky—*Tertium Organum:
The Third Canon of Thought*
ISBN 978-1-907661-47-1

Dwight Goddard—*A Buddhist Bible*
ISBN 978-1-907661-44-0

Michael Tymn—*The Afterlife Revealed*
ISBN 978-1-970661-90-7

Michael Tymn—*Transcending the
Titanic: Beyond Death's Door*
ISBN 978-1-908733-02-3

Guy L. Playfair—*If This Be Magic*
ISBN 978-1-907661-84-6

Guy L. Playfair—*The Flying Cow*
ISBN 978-1-907661-94-5

Guy L. Playfair —*This House is Haunted*
ISBN 978-1-907661-78-5

Carl Wickland, M.D.—
Thirty Years Among the Dead
ISBN 978-1-907661-72-3

John E. Mack—*Passport to the Cosmos*
ISBN 978-1-907661-81-5

Peter & Elizabeth Fenwick—
The Truth in the Light
ISBN 978-1-908733-08-5

Erlendur Haraldsson—
Modern Miracles
ISBN 978-1-908733-25-2

Erlendur Haraldsson—
At the Hour of Death
ISBN 978-1-908733-27-6

Erlendur Haraldsson—
The Departed Among the Living
ISBN 978-1-908733-29-0

Brian Inglis—*Science and Parascience*
ISBN 978-1-908733-18-4

Brian Inglis—*Natural and Supernatural:
A History of the Paranormal*
ISBN 978-1-908733-20-7

Ernest Holmes—*The Science of Mind*
ISBN 978-1-908733-10-8

Victor & Wendy Zammit —*A Lawyer
Presents the Evidence For the Afterlife*
ISBN 978-1-908733-22-1

Casper S. Yost—*Patience
Worth: A Psychic Mystery*
ISBN 978-1-908733-06-1

William Usborne Moore—
Glimpses of the Next State
ISBN 978-1-907661-01-3

William Usborne Moore—
The Voices
ISBN 978-1-908733-04-7

John W. White—
The Highest State of Consciousness
ISBN 978-1-908733-31-3

Stafford Betty—
The Imprisoned Splendor
ISBN 978-1-907661-98-3

Paul Pearsall, Ph.D. —
Super Joy
ISBN 978-1-908733-16-0

**All titles available as eBooks, and selected titles available in Hardback and
Audiobook formats from www.whitecrowbooks.com**

CPSIA information can be obtained at www.ICGtesting.com
Printed in the USA
LVOW06s0755140714

394218LV00004B/218/P

9 781910 121306